How to Be a Baseball Mom
All the Sh!t You Need & Need to Know
Heather Dirck

HKD Creative, LLC

Table of Contents

Introduction

S o, your kid wants to play baseball. Welcome! Pull up your camping chair, beverage of choice, and wagon full of provisions. Let's chat.

First, I know the title says this is a book for baseball moms. And it is! But if you're a dad, grandma, cool aunt, or someone else with a youth baseball player you're running around and cheering on, pull up your chair, too.

A confession: I never really liked baseball. I know, I know. But that's where I started. It was fine to go to an MLB game on a sunny summer day for a hot dog and an overpriced beer, but I was usually bored and ready to go by sometime in the fifth inning. Guy throws a ball. Other guy tries to hit the ball. There was more throwing, some running. It all felt kind of pedantic and slow and I had trouble paying attention. Perhaps (likely...) because I didn't really understand the game, and at the time didn't really care to.

I'm all for kids playing multiple sports. Developing different muscle groups, meeting new friends, all of that. So, when mine wanted to try baseball, I agreed with a sigh. Now, a few years later, while they still play soccer, and basketball, and run track, and do other stuff... I'm all in for baseball.

I wrote this book to share the love that I developed for this sport, and to help other new baseball moms get there faster than I did. Baseball provided an incredibly rich experience for our family, particularly after we crossed over into competitive play. We've developed so many amazing friendships with team families, experienced new places together, and my kids have benefitted from amazing mentors and role models in their coaches. I can't imagine our lives without it.

All that said... **it's a LOT** and it can be overwhelming at times. Years into my baseball momming tenure, I still find myself learning new tidbits all the time. So, I wanted to capture my experience as a newbie baseball mom, what I love about it, and some of the lessons I learned along the way, in case they may be helpful to anyone else navigating this road. I didn't know what I didn't know so, really, **I'm writing the book I wanted and needed when we got started**.

⚾ ⚾ ⚾

There's something special about this baseball world. Maybe it draws from the game itself, with its structure requiring achievements to move the game forward, rather than just time running away on the game clock. Maybe it draws from the history, the sense of nostalgia of "America's Pastime" - peanuts and Cracker Jack, Babe Ruth and Jackie Robinson, warm summer evenings at the ballpark with fireworks on the Fourth of July. Maybe it's because, with 162 MLB games per team in a season, compared with 17 NFL games or even 82 NBA games, the sport runs in the background and keeps us company from the start of spring training in February through the World Series Championship in October or November.

So, what does it mean to be a baseball mom?

Like most cohorts/herds/street gangs, the glue between us moms is the shared experiences. It's huddling together under blankets and umbrellas at games. It's celebrating victory with cocktails in plastic hotel bathroom cups around a pool in Phoenix or Omaha. It's collaborative learning of the game (to help people like me who didn't really understand it) so that we can all be fully present and engaged. It's sharing Band-Aids or ice packs when someone gets banged up sliding into second, informing each other what the score or the count is if GameChanger is lagging, or capturing photos of special moments to share with a fellow mom who couldn't be there that day. It's really just being there side-by-side to support our kids – all of them. We spend a lot of time together, become a tribe, and, while we may sometimes have differing objectives, depending on what jersey our kid is wearing and which dugout their stuff is currently scattered around in, we are part of a larger sisterhood.

We're the planners, the schedulers, the know-which-jersey-to-wearers, the get-everyone's-tail-feather-out-of-the-house-on-timers, the taxi drivers, the travel agents, the cheerleaders, the consolers, the nurses, the scorekeepers, the photographers, the constant source of food, and the magical removers of grass stains and RED dirt from WHITE pants (WHY ARE THEY WHITE????). And, like most things in motherhood, **we do it all with the ultimate goal of our kids learning to do all those things - and so much more - *for themselves* as young adults.** And, well, because baseball is fun!

Baseball, like other sports, offers so many teaching moments.

We all want our kids to experience joy and success! Like most moms, I also want my kids to encounter challenges that will help them grow. I want them to experience age-appropriate adversity and failure. I want them to learn to be gracious with others experiencing defeat. And I want them to comprehend through their sometimes-thick skulls that honing skills and becoming talented at something takes work. Actual work that requires time and effort and open-mindedness to coaching and new information. A half-assed attitude of I'll-practice-when-I-feel-like-it-because-I-already-know-how-to-do-that-mom won't do the trick.

We want them to figure out how to manage and learn from challenges while in a safe space, and baseball can provide that. How many strikes they threw or how many hits they got on June 23 when they were 12 years old = who cares when they're 18 or 25 or

43. But what they learned from the experience (I didn't throw/hit well on Saturday = I should get feedback from Coach and practice more) may matter a lot. We also want our kids to know it's not the end of the world if they don't make every play and if things don't always go their way. We want them to know how to deal with it in a healthy way, to be able to accept it, and move forward acknowledging the learning and growth. With the right coaches walking alongside them, and the right support from us, they can get all of that from baseball. I mean, it is a game of failure. Hall of Fame batters get hits about ⅓ of the time. It makes the wins and achievements feel earned and all the more sweet.

Maybe most importantly, it's the time together.

While I may indulge in grouching about getting up and out the door at o'dark thirty to drive an hour across town for the 6:45 a.m. warm up before the 8:00 a.m. game, I absolutely cherish those early morning car rides with my son. It's quiet and feels like most of the world is still asleep, and the day feels fresh. It's calm, without the mourning or celebration that will color the ride home. It amazes me how much I can learn from him during those rides. Definitely about the game ("So, why was Jimmy out at third yesterday when he'd already crossed home to score?"). But also just about other stuff going in his life. Without that time and space, I don't know when those conversations would happen amid the hustle and bustle. I'm grateful for them, and I wish for these precious moments of connection for all my fellow moms. And, even if they'd never admit it, and may not realize it themselves for a few years or decades, I know our presence and support in their baseball experience means a lot to our kids, too.

So, what should you expect from this book?

We'll try to cover all the bases (ha!). Whether your kid is young and you're trying to figure out how to get started, they've been playing for a while and want to play at a higher level, or the universe conspired to drop them onto a team and you need to figure out what to do next, we'll get there. The experience of this game evolves as your kid does, so in three to five years you may be looking to get something different from this book than you are today.

What do you need, need to know, and need to do to be a baseball mom? We'll go over:

- How to find the right team for the upcoming season

- Understanding this game you'll be watching

- What your player needs (A lot. They need a lot.)

- Scheduling: from annual planning, to season flow, to games and tournaments

- Game Day: from getting ready and packing up to where to sit and the post-game car ride

- Traveling with the team

- How to budget and pay for all this sh!t

- Peeking over the fence at what's beyond youth baseball

- How to clean the #&@*!!! white pants

- A glossary translating weird stuff people say at baseball games

Let's get started.

Chapter 1
Getting Started: Finding a Team & What to Expect

All the Flavors of Youth Baseball

L ead off task: a player needs a team. This step can seem easy (just sign up online with the local league, duh) or agonizingly overwhelming (heaven help me with all the options and levels with their multiple A's and I'm-not-sure-what-I'm-looking-for-but-feel-like-I'm-missing-something circus).

The baseball world is huge - there are organizations and leagues and divisions and clubs galore, with opportunities for kids to participate at any age and level. With so many options, it may feel like a full-time job to sort through it all.

But, the baseball world is also small - there is a remarkable network among baseball people that can be tapped into for advice and leads on teams once you take the red pill and start navigating the Matrix.

We were fortunate in that a lot of our family's baseball experiences fell into our lap, with more-knowledgeable friends texting us registration links or information about tryouts so our kids could play together. It worked great for us, and it was so much fun to spend time at the ballpark with friends - both for the kids and for the parents. However, when the time came that I needed to find teams on my own, I found there was a bit of a learning curve.

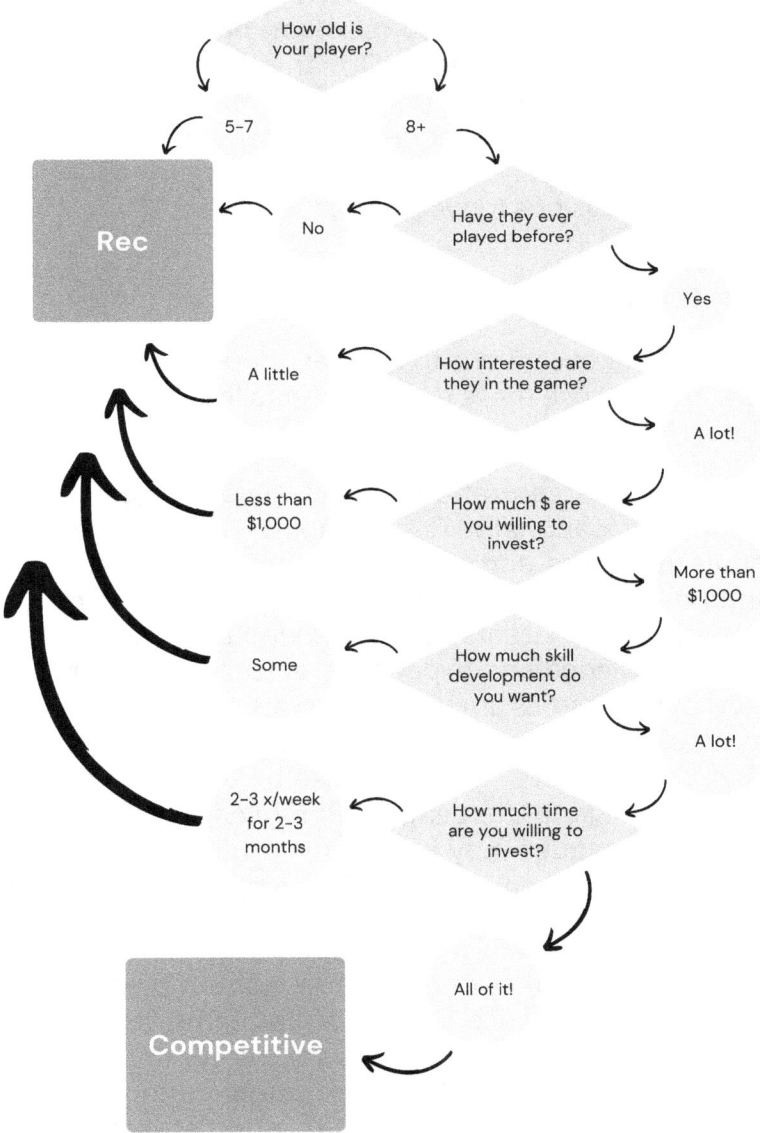

While each family and player is different, running through the questions in the flow chart above may help with orientation and narrowing the options, whether your kid is just getting started or if they're at a crossroads. Also, please know that **all the estimates of cost and league descriptions and potential dates in this**

chapter are just that – *estimates* intended to provide general guideposts and a relative comparison between the different options. Because there are SO many different organizations running youth baseball programs, there could be (wide) variations in dates and costs and other details, depending on what's in your area. Please always check with your local organization(s) before making final decisions for your family.

A few definitions

While there are exceptions to and variations of every definition, I understand and use these words in the following way throughout this book:

League = An organization that facilitates gameplay in a community or nationally. They establish rules, organize teams, schedule practices and games, get permits to use school or community fields, and provide umpires. Coaches are typically volunteers: often parents of players who have varying levels of baseball knowledge and experience. A league may have its own teams that play games among themselves, and/or they may serve as an umbrella that coordinates play among several community baseball organizations. They may also be affiliated with national organizations like Little League, Pony League, the Babe Ruth League, etc. Leagues may be run for profit or as a non-profit. They may have recreational and/or competitive teams in their organization.

Club = Often a smaller organization with its own indoor, and maybe outdoor, practice facility for its teams. Its primary role is recruiting and training players for competitive teams that participate in externally organized games and tournaments, though some may host their own tournaments, too. Coaches may be parents or not, and typically have more extensive baseball knowledge and experience. Clubs are usually for-profit organizations.

Independent Team = These are formed when one or more coaches, often but not always parents who have baseball knowledge and experience, decide to establish a team and recruit their own players. They operate outside of any organization, find their own practice space, and register to participate in tournaments and/or leagues for games.

Levels, Classifications, and Divisions

Youth baseball is sliced and diced into different levels and divisions, and it can help to understand the terminology and differing opportunities when searching for a team. The first narrowing factor will be your player's age. Got a 5-year-old? They'll play tee-ball, and that's pretty much only offered through recreational leagues. Got a 9-, 10-, or 11-year-old, particularly one with a few years of experience under their belt, a bit of skill, and the desire to learn and play more? That's when the real search begins.

Age

The first step before registration is to understand your player's "baseball age" for your league. While there will always be some element of beefcakes and little guys playing together, like all sports, age cutoffs put a lid on the size and strength differences due to physical maturity among players in the same class. In some rec leagues, age divisions may be made by a player's grade in school. In competitive or tournament baseball, age divisions are usually made by a birth date cutoff, so expect to provide a copy of your player's birth certificate for the team to have on file to prove it. There may still be times at a game of 12- or 13-year-olds when you'd swear one of the opposing players could have driven themselves there or bought a beer for the coach, but the leagues and tournaments do try to keep things fair.

In baseball, the number included in the titling of an age division is _inclusive of_ the maximum age by a date determined in the league/tournament rules. So, for example, 12U means players **12**-years-old **AND Under**. Some other sports define this differently (in our local soccer league, 12U meant you had to be under and not yet 12, which made things fun and confusing for a minute). There is not one standard age cutoff date for youth baseball, so make sure to verify your local organization's age rules when registering or trying out, but here are a couple common dates used by major organizations:

April 30 = USA Baseball, USSSA (United States Specialty Sports Association), and the Babe Ruth League

- For example, for 12U, a player must be 12 or under <u>through April 30 of the baseball season in question</u> (flip to the Scheduling chapter for more on season timing). A player's age at the time you're signing them up or trying out is irrelevant. So, if a player turns 13 on April 30 or earlier, they are too old and need to be on a 13U team for that season. But, if they turn 13 on May 1 (so, they're still 12 on April 30), they can play on a 12U team.

August 31 = Little League

- In this league, the players in each age division are a bit younger than what's described above, as they can't have a birthday until later in/after the season. Keeping with our 12U example, a player can't turn 13 until September 1 the year of their 12U season.

Most leagues will allow kids to play up - meaning they can play with kids who are a bit older than them. This can be a good option for kids who are big for their age, kids who are extra talented for their age, and/or kids who just want the challenge of playing with older kids. They just can't play down, as that would give them an unfair advantage.

Divisions

Leagues all have slightly different ways of describing and subdividing the levels of play for different ages, particularly in the younger years. Like all things, the details will vary a bit in the league closest to you, but here's a general overview.

Step 1: Tee-ball (a.k.a. T-ball)

- If your kid is 5 and under, or up to 7ish and has never played before, this is the best place to start.

- The ball sits there for the batter on a tee, so it has no movement when they try to hit it.

- There is no pitcher... unless your league doesn't do straight tee-ball, and combines with coach pitch, as described in Step 2.

Step 2: Coach-led pitching

- Age range: if your kid is 5-7 and has played at least one season of tee-ball, and/or hasn't played tee-ball but is between 7ish and 9ish, they'll play at this level.

- This step - the land between tee-ball and kid-pitch - is a little squishy and varies the most from league to league. The options for ball delivery (below) could be divided into more than one level, happen in a different order, and/or your league could skip one of these types of play.

- There is no opposing "pitcher" per se, but the ball is (usually) moving when the batter takes a swing. Options include:

  ○ Coach pitch - when a player's own coach throws the ball for them to try to hit. Possible tee-as-backup, if the batter isn't able to get a hit after X number of throws by the coach.

  ○ Machine pitch - when a player's own coach operates a ball-throwing device from the pitcher's mound

Step 3: Player pitch

- Age range: starting at 8-10 years old, and onward

- The pitcher is a player on the opposing team.

- This starts to look more like "real" baseball. Some of the training wheels come off, with no more tees or coaches on the field to pitch or run a machine.

When going online to register your player, your league may use categories like Minor League, Major League, Intermediate, Junior League, Senior League, etc. These are just labels for different age divisions and vary in how they're used. Just look for age and skill requirements for a level and go from there.

A quick web search for "youth baseball near me" can give you a general lay of the land of organizations in your area, and will provide more than enough options when getting started. The results will likely include organizations from recreational leagues to clubs, and we'll walk through how they're different below. But, know that **the search won't be all-inclusive, though this may not matter unless you have a more advanced player and are in search of a new team**. We'll discuss deeper searching in the competitive section below.

For the purposes of simplicity, I've divided descriptions of the types of baseball organizations and experiences into Recreational and Competitive. **The separating factor I used is whether kids can just sign up and play (Recreational) or whether a player has to try out (Competitive)**. Deciding which of these experiences is the right fit is the first step.

Recreational (Rec)

This is a great option when kids are young, when they are venturing into baseball for the first time, and/or for kids who are older and like to play baseball more casually. Rec leagues may be run through city, town, or county parks and recreation departments, through non-profits like the YMCA, or through independent local leagues.

Depending on your kid's level of interest in playing and/or your family's bandwidth, you could hang out on rec teams forever and have a great time. It's lower cost, less time commitment, easier to sign up to play together with friends, and typically easier to find closer to home. While there will still be plenty of excitement, nail-biting, disappointment, and glory, it feels lower-stakes and more accessible than more competitive teams. Our boys both spent years playing on rec teams. They had a lot of fun, made new friends, and developed a basic understanding of the game and how it's played.

Frankly, for years, rec was all I knew of baseball or of any other youth sport. It was enough, and it was great. You can hop online, find a league with a location and calendar that works for you, and register. A few weeks or months later, you'll find out who your coach will be and where to show up for the first practice. Done.

I was vaguely aware that other options were out there, but when friends who were more dialed into the baseball world than me started talking about things like "competitive" and "club teams" my eyes kind of glazed over. I was almost totally unfamiliar with that part of youth sports and, frankly, didn't have any interest in pursuing it. Investing thousands of dollars and seemingly every free moment of our summer into a kid's sport sounded crazy and terrible (oh the irony...). We wanted to go camping, to travel to places other than baseball fields, to have leisurely weekends to see friends and, if we must, do yard work. Without something different knocking on our door and falling into our lap when it did, we may have very well, and happily, stayed in rec.

Note that some rec leagues will have assessments for new players. This isn't a try-out per se, meaning admittance to the league is not based on performance. Assessments give the coaches a feel for the skill level of the new kids, so that each team picks up a combo of more-skilled and less-skilled new players. This helps even out the competitiveness of teams.

Rec All Star

Sometimes a rec league will have All Star teams. What this means can vary a lot from league to league, and a single league may have various All Star or other higher-level options in addition to its primary program of "regular" rec teams. All Star teams could be short-lived add-ons, meaning that players may be nominated by coaches mid-season, or selected through tryouts, to play a tournament or two with an All Star team in addition to their regular league play with their primary team. Or, these teams could run more like a competitive program, with pre-season tryouts to select a team that will play together for a whole season, both within the league and in out-of-league tournaments. There is the potential to travel with a rec All Star team, either for planned trips to one or more tournaments, or due to earned achievement. For example, if the team plays well and ranks high at a state-level tournament, they may earn their way into regionals or nationals, which are likely hosted in another state.

Recreational (Rec) at a Glance

- **Tryouts?** - No

- **Ages / Levels** - Tee-ball and up

- **Playing time** - Should theoretically be equal for all players. Rec ball is supposed to be for learning and fun!

- **Approximate cost** - $250-$1,000 per season, including uniform items and new gear if needed

- **Approximate season length** - 2-3 months

- **Skill development** - Minimal/basic, dependent on the coach

- **Practices** - 1-2 per week

- **Games** - 1-2 per week; 8-15ish in a season

Competitive (Travel/Club/Tournament Ball)

This is where things get real. The tryouts. The selection (or not) process. The sacrifice of all free time and disposable income. Competitive baseball. It becomes a defining aspect of life for not only the player but the whole family. It is huge and demanding and families should enter competitive sports with clear eyes about the commitment. It is not for everyone. This was the kind of youth sports I studiously avoided for years, but it has become an intrinsic and amazing part of my kids' lives, and I've fallen in love with it along the way.

When is it worth it? If your **player** really loves the game. That is the most important thing. Not that mom or dad or grandpa loves the game. While it's fantastic to have family that is excited and supportive, it can't be the driver for playing at the competitive level. If your **player** doesn't **really** love it and have the desire to learn, the motivation to practice and develop skills, to be challenged, to play a lot more games in a season than they did in rec, and to spend a lot of time with the sport (like, several nights a week for **at least** half the year, and most of every weekend for four to five months), competitive baseball may not be a good fit. It's a question you may want to revisit at the end of each season before recommitting to the same team or attending tryouts for another one. If they're not happy playing, if they're not excited about it and (at least most days) looking forward to practices and games, it's a recipe for misery. Cut and run, and consider playing at the rec level if they just want to dial it back. Or, find a different sport or activity that will bring them and the family joy. Youth baseball should be fun, not a job!

But, if and when they're ready for it and want it, and the family is willing and able to go along for the ride, it can be pretty amazing. It's extra amazing when you're on a great team! Note that a team being great is sometimes, but not necessarily always, the same thing as a team with on-field success. Winning is - of course! - aimed for, practiced for, sometimes expected, and always fantastic. But it could be argued that it might not be the most important thing. A great team, for me, is a group of players my son wants to spend time with, a group of families my family wants to spend time with (because spend a lot of time with them you will), and coaches (!!!) who are 1) good people who 2) know, love, and respect the game, 3) know how to teach it and are willing to invest the time to do so, and 4) build positive connections with the players while helping them improve their skill set, both on and off the field.

So, what is the right age for a player to go competitive? It really depends upon the player and the family. There are those of the mindset that a kid who loves and has a knack for baseball should get on board with a competitive program as soon as possible to develop their skills and mechanics in the right way from the start, and not have to retrain bad habits. Others have the mindset that playing too much baseball too young can lead to mental burnout and a loss of love for the game, as well as physical damage due to overuse, particularly of a pitcher's throwing arm. And some are of the mindset that playing at the competitive level isn't ever necessary for a player to have success in high school and beyond.

Some indications that playing on a competitive team could be a good next step are 1) if your player wants more baseball (practices and games) than is available at the rec level, and/or 2) if your player is skilled and would like to play on a team with similarly-skilled teammates. Our sons both moved from rec to competitive when they were entering 11U. For us, that was the season that bridged the end of elementary school (spring of 5th grade) into the summer before middle school, which starts at 6th grade in our district. It's what worked for us - they were excited and ready for it at the time, and with the imminent "graduation" to a different school, it felt like a time of transition. They were considered a bit behind other players who started playing competitively earlier and had more training and skills development than our kids. But, it's definitely possible to not only catch up once a green/raw player starts to get that training, but to have them become a leader on the team. It's the right time for your player when it's the right time for your player.

Something we didn't do initially (because we didn't know about or consider it) but that could ease a later transition from rec to competitive - or even from rec to high school ball - would be to regularly participate in skills training camps and/or one-on-one coaching. Many clubs, and sometimes high schools, offer camps or clinics in the offseason (usually fall) that are open to anyone in the community. You don't have to be on one of their teams to register. Same thing for individual coaching - you can find this year round, but **the best time to make adjustments to mechanics is in the offseason**. While there is a cost, it is less than a full commitment to a competitive team, and can be a great benefit for aspiring ball players.

Competitive at a Glance

- **Tryouts?** - Yes

- **Ages/levels** - 8U and up, with some training opportunities for younger kids

- **Playing time** - May start equal and become merit-based or may always be **merit-based**. Competitive ball should also be fun (it's baseball!), but there's more of a focus at this level on performance and winning games, so playing time is not always equal.

- **Approximate cost - $3,000-$1,000,000** (Kidding. Kind of.) - **See the Chapter 7 for more detail on finances, budgeting worksheets, and fundraising ideas**, but for a **quick glance:**

  - Registration: $500-$3,500+ per season *just for team/league/club registration.* Registration fees will be on the lower end for an independent or league competitive team; clubs will be on the higher end.

- Team/Tournament Fees: $800-$3,000+ (this is different than and in addition to the registration fee)

- Uniform Items: $200-$500ish

- Equipment/Gear: $300-$1,000+

- If playing at this level, you may want to register for off-season skills camps ($100-$1,500+) and/or individual coaching ($50-$100ish/hour) for hitting or pitching.

- Traveling? Estimate $250-$5,000+ per trip, depending on how far you're going, for how long, with how many family members.

- $5-10 per week in lottery tickets to dream about covering everything above.

- **Approximate season length**

  - 2-6 months of off- to pre-season training

  - 4-6 months of in-season training and games. Some teams may play year-round, but most don't.

- **Skill development** - moderate to sophisticated, depending on the league/club/coach

- **Practices** - 2-4+ per week

- **Games** - 3-8 per week; 40-80+ in a season

Experiences in Competitive Baseball Land come in a LOT of different shapes and sizes. There are league teams that play league games but also some tournaments. There are club and independent teams that exclusively play tournaments. There are club and independent teams that play in tournaments but also join a league for extra games. There are teams that may play only in local tournaments. There are teams that travel one, two, or three times a season. There are teams that burn up the pavement and the skies traveling every week or two. But, one way or another, competitive teams always: require tryouts, provide much more player training and development, and play in tournaments.

An important note on club teams: they are not all the same. Each club has a different philosophy, culture, and reputation, so it is worthwhile to do some research on which one(s) may be the best fit for your player before trying out and locking in. Some clubs are pretty overcrowded, which can limit facility access due to an emphasis on profit (squeezing in more teams) over player development and customer service. And within each club, the experience can vary a lot from team to team, depending both on the club structure and individual coaches. Some clubs may have one flagship team, which gets a lot of attention and resources, and a bunch of "other" teams, which may or may not serve as feeders for the "good" team. As was mentioned earlier, and as will be mentioned again, **the most important factor in player experience is the coach(es) for your team**.

Tournaments

Weekend tournaments can be weird to get used to if you're accustomed to rec baseball (or other rec sports), which is almost exclusively league play. By league play, I mean a series of pre-scheduled independent games. We'll get more into what this looks like in the Scheduling chapter. But, generally speaking, expect that every weekend is a separate tournament.

Typically, teams will play **two pool play games on Saturday**, the outcome of which establishes seeding for **bracket play on Sunday**. Most weekend tournaments are single elimination, so when they lose a game on Sunday, they're done. But, **if they win, they keep playing - potentially up to three or four games that day.** Hope you brought snacks!

Tournaments are usually independent of each other, but may affect seeding at an end of season tournament within that particular organization. Some tournaments may be longer than two days and have more pool play and/or double elimination brackets. They can be a long weekend of three to four days, or last up to a week.

Finding Tryouts

Does competitive sound right for your player? Great! Time to try out.

In some parts of the country, organizations will host their main public tryouts for the following season near the end of, or just after, the current season, often between late-June and early-August. Other places hold tryouts later in the fall or even in early winter. Whatever time of year it happens, organizations in the same community typically have their main, open-door tryouts around the same time because they are competing with each other for the same pool of players.

I've heard this month or so when most organizations hold their tryouts called 'silly season', and that it is. This is when teams invite back (or not) their current players for the next year. It's also when players who are unhappy with their team look for new opportunities, but they may not want to burn the connection with their current team until they have a new spot locked down. And teams may be a little cagey during tryouts about the number of openings they have for new players, and about when they'll get back with you, if they are waiting for firm commitment (= a signed contract and $$$) from existing players for the upcoming season. It's kind of a cross between a chicken and egg situation and getting a non-committal response from a potential prom date who's waiting for a better offer.

In case your community has tryouts about six months before official team training starts in January, **start your research as early as you can**. When testing a search engine recently to see what popped up in my area, most major organizations were included, at least when I zoomed in enough on the map. But, smaller organizations and independent teams were not. For the major organizations, just check their website to see when they're holding tryouts for your age group, register if required, and put it on the calendar. **Some tryouts you can just show up for** and sign in with info about your player when you arrive. **Other tryouts require you to register and reserve a slot in advance. Some tryouts are free, other organizations charge a fee (often $25-$50, but sometimes more) to try out**.

Going down the rabbit hole into social media groups for youth baseball in your community, as well as personal networking, can reveal other opportunities. I had no idea what I didn't know until, during a conversation with a potential coach, he repeatedly said, "You can find it on the Facebook group," like I would know what he was talking about. So, I pretended I knew what he was talking about and, later that day, searched for Facebook groups about youth baseball in our area.

Lo and behold! The not-so-secret society was revealed. There were independent coaches advertising tryouts, clubs advertising still-open positions (months after public tryouts were over), parents searching for late tryouts and getting specific leads and contacts in comments on their post, people seeking and sharing recommendations on great hitting or pitching coaches in specific parts of town, funny baseball memes, and more.

Like all things on social media, reader beware. But I was amazed at all the jockeying and action happening seemingly under the radar of what was posted on organization websites. There is a treasure trove of advice, mostly good but sometimes questionable or self-serving, available to anyone asking a question.

Baseball can also have a bit of a who-you-know element, with friends and contacts sharing otherwise unadvertised opportunities and making introductions between potential players and coaches.

Take that red pill, ask around, and may the force be with you.

What Tryouts Are Like

At the cattle-call public tryouts with larger organizations, expect a lot of kids, coaches with clipboards, and activity. Plan to get there at least 15-20 minutes before the advertised start to allow time to check in and get oriented before they kick things off. If you have an old jersey with your kid's name on the back, that can be helpful for identification by prospective coaches. If you don't have one, no worries - they'll probably give them a number to wear either way.

They'll run the kids through different skill areas in groups, rotating through a speed test, a fielding test or two (for grounders and fly balls), a hitting test, and maybe pitching or catching. Expect to be there for an hour or two. Don't expect to get an answer that day; it will probably be at least a few days, often longer, before you hear anything. There are often (a lot) more kids trying out than there are available spots on rosters. For that reason, **it can be a good idea to attend tryouts at multiple organizations**. Some organizations send nice "thanks for coming but we've filled our roster" rejections; others may just ghost the players they don't choose. It's not uncommon for organizations to string prospective players along for weeks as they wait for confirmations - or not - from their first choices.

Sometimes you may get a more personal tryout if you find a team with an open slot after the main tryout wave is over. Coaches often call this a workout, but it's a tryout. It can feel a little less overwhelming in some ways due to less crowds, hubbub, and formality. But it can also feel more intimidating, as your kid may be alone in the spotlight. It may just be one or two kids with the coach doing some skills and drills (fielding, hitting, and maybe pitcher or catcher work, if that's what they're looking for), or the prospective player(s) may join the rest of the team for a practice or two so the coaches can get a look at them and see if it will be a good fit. You should get an answer much sooner in this scenario. Maybe even that day.

Classifications

All competitive/tournament teams, and some leagues, use classifications to identify their level of skill or experience. Teams may self-classify when they register for tournaments, or they may be classified by a tournament director based on prior performance. If a team over- or under-performs its self-classification in prior tournaments, a tournament director may re-classify them to a higher or lower level to try to even-out competition (which means more fun for everyone), reduce blow-outs, and stymie the damn trophy hunters (asshole higher-level teams that register for a lower-level tournament just to win).

There are two common classification scales that may be used interchangeably or jointly: AA-Major and D1-D3. Some organizations also throw in bronze / silver / gold / rookie / elite / advanced / bologna, all of which we're going to ignore here because they are commonly understood modifiers, add unnecessarily to the word salad we already have, may be used inconsistently, and/or don't matter.

Scale 1 - Team classification

- AA: Pronounced double-A. This classification is for beginning-level teams and may comprise more than half of all teams. The term 'single A' is rarely used, but would be lower than AA, referring to rec-level teams. AA teams play in mostly local tournaments and may have a record of .500 or less.

- AAA: Pronounced triple-A. These are mid-level teams and comprise maybe ⅓ of all competitive teams. These teams have probably played together in prior seasons, have a strong winning record against AA teams, and at least a .500 record against other teams of the same level.

- Majors: These are the strongest, most experienced teams, and there are fewer of them - maybe 10% of all teams. They often seek out the best competition at local or out-of-state tournaments and have a strong winning record against AAA and AA teams.

Scale 2 - Division classification

- D1: Division 1 = Majors and high-performing AAA teams

- D2: Division 2 = Mid to High AA teams and mid to low AAA teams

- D3: Division 3 = New or lower performing AA teams, other beginning-level teams

Fall Ball

Fall ball is kind of bonus baseball. It's an extra, separate season played after the primary season wraps up for the year. It's usually seen as a time for development and practice in preparation for the main spring-summer season. A lot of youth baseball players take the fall off from baseball to play another sport, like soccer, football, or basketball. This gives their throwing arms a break after a long season, and can increase cardio training and develop other muscle groups to become a more well-rounded athlete. My older son, who catches and plays outfield, plays soccer in the off season; his baseball coach loves it because it keeps his legs strong and his speed up. But each family will decide what's best for them. Some love baseball so much they want to continue playing whenever they can!

How to Find a Team

First Steps by Team Type

Rec

- Just Google to find leagues in the area and sign up!

- If your kid has a friend they want to play with, you can often request to be placed on the same team when registering.

- If your kid has a friend or group of friends already playing with the league, you may be able to contact their coach to inquire about being placed on that team.

- Look to see if the league holds assessments for new players and put that on the calendar.

Rec All Star

- **There could be tryouts for an All Star team in your league - if so, look for dates if your player is interested.**

- Participants could be nominated by coaches - maybe one or two players per team. If this is the case, players can't seek out the team. The team will find the players.

Competitive/Travel

- Research clubs, leagues, and independent teams and note

their tryout dates.

- Start looking in May or June to play on a team the following spring/summer.

- Sign up for tryout slot(s) in advance, if required.

- Plan to try out with at least 3-5 teams/clubs, especially if this is your player's first venture into competitive baseball. They may only need one, but it can be educational to see what's out there.

- Ask your people for leads on teams: former coaches, former teammates, family, and friends.

- Check social media groups: look for advertised formal tryouts or post-tryout-season "workouts" to fill in late gaps. These groups can be especially helpful in finding independent teams in your area, which are often invisible when doing a general web search.

- Make a list or spreadsheet to keep track of everything above, because it's a lot.

- You're going to start feeling like a sports agent and wonder where your commission is.

Dialing it in

Here are some things to research, ask the coaches about during/after tryouts, and consider before signing on the dotted line. This can be a helpful exercise whether you're in the fortunate position to have more than one option before committing to a team, or when reflecting on your experience at the end of a season and evaluating whether to stay with the same team next year or shop around for a new one.

- **Gut check** - Does it feel right?

- **Budget and logistics**

~ What are the registration fees, uniform fees, and team/tournament/travel fees?
~ How many tournaments will the team play?
~ How much will the team travel, and to where?

- **Roster size -** A roster size of 11-12ish is about right in youth baseball. High schools and some elite teams carry more players. You need nine players to field a team, and having a few extras is helpful to cover times when injuries, illnesses, and family vacations happen, or when someone needs a coach-determined rest or time out. But, the more extra players there are on a team, the less playing time there is to go around and more people will be sitting on the bench for more innings.

- **Opportunity for growth**
~ What is the coach(es)' baseball background/experience?
~ What is their training and development program for players?
~ How many days per week are invested in skill-building and practice, for how many hours, focusing on what?
~ If the team is part of a club, will you have access to the facility and/or coaching outside of formal team practices?

- **Connection with coaches** - This is more relevant when reevaluating whether to stay with a team, but may also come into play if you have the chance to interact or meet with coaches during the team selection process. Do they click with your player? Is there something about their personality or coaching style that you really like and respect? Or the opposite? Coaches are integral not only to your child's experience in baseball, but can be one of the most important role models in their life.

When we first ventured into competitive baseball, one of the reasons we decided to overcommit our schedule and vomit out the money for playing on a club team is because of our initial conversation with the coaches. I loved how they incorporated beyond-baseball learning lessons and personal growth in their coaching style - things like time management, personal responsibility, accepting feedback, and valuing hard work over raw talent. Baseball players are built, not born, as they say.

You want someone who will challenge your kid. Not someone who is a constant yeller or always angry, but someone who is going to inspire them to work harder, to want to impress the coach with their effort and resulting success. Someone who loves the game and is willing to invest the time and patience to help their players improve. Someone who will hold them accountable with reasonable and proportional consequences when they make mistakes, whether on the field or as a teammate. Someone who will encourage them and provide a role model of how to be a good sport, both in victory and in defeat. If my kid is doing something wrong, or could be doing something better, I want their coach (or their teacher, or any other trusted adult in their life) to identify it and help them learn. I may be describing a unicorn coach (or just ours), but, at the end of the day, we want our kids to spend time with people who we believe will be a positive influence on their young lives.

Some additional questions to consider on the coaches and team dynamic include:
~ What's the club and/or coaches' general philosophy and goals for the players, practices, and games?
~ Will the team largely stay together from year to year, or should you expect major changes in teammates and coaches each season?
~ Are the coach(es) parents of kids on the team or not?
~ **Most importantly, why are the coaches coaching**? For the money? For the love of it? Because they have a kid on the team?

• **Daddy ball issues?** - Many coaches, from rec to club, are the parent of a player on the team. They have the most baked-in buy-in to dedicate the time and energy it takes to coach. We've had some amazing coaches who had a son (or daughter!) on the team, so **just because the coach is a parent does not mean there will be issues like this**. But we've also experienced "daddy ball".

Daddy ball happens when the kid(s) of one or more of the coaches regularly get a disproportionate amount of playing time and/or key positions. If their kid is a stud, the playing time and positioning feels more logical and forgivable, especially at higher levels. But it's crazy frustrating if their kid rarely takes a turn sitting an inning out, is always in the top half of the batting order, and/or always plays in key positions despite having an equivalent or lower skill level than their teammates. It's hard to watch your team losing a game because a coach's kid is making tons of errors but isn't being pulled out and replaced like any other player on the team would be in that situation. It can be difficult to identify this until you are on a team and start to see the pattern during actual games. But, as you're exploring your options, have your antennae up for this.

One way to avoid this is with a paid coach through a club, who does not have a kid on the team and is coaching for the love of the game rather than for family obligation. While there are both great and less-than-great paid coaches who may or may not check all the other boxes you're looking for in this important role, at least daddy ball is taken off the table as a risk.

- **Is your kid having fun?** - Is it going to be fun **every** day? No. There will be hard practices, difficult losses, hitting slumps, run-ins with disrespectful opponents, disagreements with coaches and teammates. It's life. Stuff happens. No team, coach, or player is perfect. But, on balance, is your kid having fun? Do they like their coaches and teammates? Do they enjoy playing and look forward to practices and games? Do you see them smiling and laughing with teammates? Getting fired up and excited? If your kid is getting burned out or dreads going to practice or games, it may be time to reevaluate.

- **Gut check again** - It's first, last, and most important.

Chapter 2
Baseball 101: The Game, the Positions, the Rules

B aseball is everywhere. It's woven into the fabric of American culture so intrinsically that we reference it without thinking about it. We step up to the plate when we take on a responsibility at work. Striking out when we blow it. Hitting it out of the park when we do a great job. We're batting a thousand (1.000) when we're perfect at something. We keep our eye on the ball when we need to focus on something important. We got to 2nd or 3rd base with that date in high school. ;) Baseball surrounds us.

Despite all that, while I understood the basics of the game, I had a lot to learn. I found that I had so much more appreciation of MLB games after watching and learning from my kids and their teammates, picking up rules and nuances along the way. I recently sat next to a mom during a youth game who grew up in a country where baseball isn't a major sport. It was a super fun conversation to explain the basics of what was happening in the game - and why - as our boys were out there playing together.

If your kid is going to be playing baseball, you're likely going to be watching a lot of baseball. The experience is a lot more fun and meaningful if you understand what the hell is going on. This chapter isn't intended to capture every single rule and nuance - it would be 1,000 pages long and about as engaging as the dictionary. Baseball is a rich and very situational game; there will be moments when arcane rules or unusual plays are pulled out of hats. Ask around - you won't be the only one looking for clarity, and there's likely someone in your parent section who can explain.

The intent of this chapter is to provide enough background and context so you can comfortably enjoy watching the game.

A Bit of History

The exact origin of the game is a little fuzzy.[1] Despite popular myth, it was likely *not* invented by Civil War major general Abner Doubleday in 1839 in Cooperstown, New York.[2] The Mills Commission operated from 1905-1908 with the goal of unearthing baseball's origin story.[3] However, the founder of the commission Albert Spalding - yes, the baseball equipment Spalding - really wanted the game to have purely American roots, not British ones. So, the commission hung their findings primarily on a letter to a newspaper in Denver by Abner Graves, a guy who grew up in Cooperstown and claimed to have seen Doubleday sketch out a drawing of a baseball field. Graves was five years old in 1839 while Doubleday was a 20-year-old cadet at West Point, where he studied from 1838-1842... with his only documented leave of absence in the summer of 1840.[4] Graves was also later found criminally insane while being tried for the murder of his wife, so perhaps his testimony should be taken with a bucket full of salt. Doubleday has no documented connection to the game other than ordering baseball equipment for the "amusement" of an infantry regiment in Texas in 1871, and never claimed any connection to baseball or mentioned the game in any of his 67 diaries. He was a well-known and upstanding fellow, so perhaps that's why he was picked for the honor, however misplaced and mystifying it may be?

Despite all that, the strength of this myth led to the establishment of Doubleday Field, America's "original baseball diamond", in 1920

---

1. https://www.history.com/news/who-invented-baseball

2. https://www.americanheritage.com/man-who-didnt-invent-baseball

3. http://www.catskills-house.com/images/baseball_hall_of_fame_A.pdf

4. https://sabr.org/bioproj/person/abner-doubleday

on a former cow pasture where Doubleday and schoolmates are alleged to have played 80 years prior. A businessman in Cooperstown got on the Doubleday train during the Great Depression. He leveraged the commission's report to drum up tourism and commerce in Cooperstown by establishing the National Baseball Hall of Fame and Museum there in time for "baseball's centennial" in 1939.

As the museum was ramping up to open, they received a letter from Bruce Cartwright claiming that his grandfather, Alexander Cartwright, Jr., had actually invented the modern game. Alexander Cartwright, Jr. was a founding member of the Knickerbocker (baseball) Club of New York, drew the first known diagram of a baseball field, and was on a committee that wrote the rules for modern baseball in 1845. The first documented baseball game was held on June 19, 1846 on old cricket grounds in Hoboken, New Jersey; the Knickerbockers lost 1-23 to the New York Baseball Club. You can find the scorecard from that game, Cartwright's baseball diagram and rules, and a plaque in the Hall of Fame identifying Cartwright as the "Father of Modern Baseball"... all in the National Baseball Hall of Fame and Museum in Cooperstown, about a block away from Doubleday Field. Ha. Regardless of the dodgy history, Cooperstown is a lovely place to visit, the museum is amazing, and it's a fun destination for the revered summertime baseball tournaments for 12-year-olds.

So, did Cartwright pluck baseball out of thin air? No. He modified and built on existing ball-and-stick games. The first known book referencing "base-ball" was John Newbery's *A Little Pretty Pocket-Book,* which had a poem and illustration of the game. It was originally printed in England in 1742 and reprinted in New York in 1762, more than a decade before the American Revolutionary War. There are references to "playing at base" at Valley Forge in 1778. In 1787, Princeton College banned students from playing with "balls and sticks" on the college grounds. There are also similarities between baseball and the British children's game rounders, described in *The Boy's Own Book* (1828).

After decades of amateur clubs like the Knickerbockers, the game evolved into its current form and started to see paid, professional players after the Civil War. Prior to that, there were two versions of the game: the New York version (Cartwright's), which is similar to what we see today using a hard ball, and a Massachusetts version (closer to rounders), which, while having a similar objective and rules, used a softer ball. Rather than tagging a runner to get them out, you threw the ball directly at them. Fun!

The Game

So, how do you play baseball? In a nutshell: teams take turns trying to earn **runs**. A run is earned by going around all the **bases**, in order, then touching **home plate**. Runs are usually the product of plays by more than one teammate. To start running the bases, a player's goal is to hit a ball - thrown by the other team - with a bat. They want to hit it hard enough that they can run to at least one base before the other team can tag them with the ball. While a runner is touching a base, they are safe. The defending team's goal is to get outs on the batting team. Outs are caused most often by a batter **striking out** (in short, not hitting three hittable pitches), fielders **catching** a hit ball before it touches the ground, or **tagging** a runner. Once the pitching team gets three **outs** on the batting team, it's their turn to hit. The teams will alternate a set number of times, after which the team with the most runs wins. This description is oversimplified and leaves out a lot. Ready for a bunch of details and nuances and exceptions and strategies, because that's what baseball is all about? Let's dive in.

Game Structure

A game is divided into **innings**. During an inning, each team will play both offense (batting) and defense (pitching and fielding). The order in which they play those roles depends on whether they are the home or away team. The home team plays defense in the **'top' (first half) of an inning**, and offense in the **'bottom' (second half) of the inning**. This is an advantage for the home team, as they will always get the last at bats, a final opportunity to score more runs before the end of the game.

The length of an inning is not dependent on time in the way halves, periods, or quarters are in football, basketball, soccer, hockey, etc. They can be fast or slow, depending on the efficiency of the defense. A half inning ends when the defending team earns three outs, for a total of six outs per inning (three per team).

In the MLB, there are nine innings in a standard game, with extra innings if there is a tie. Youth baseball plays fewer innings (thank God). Leagues and tournaments will set rules for minimum and maximum innings, as well as "game times" for different ages.

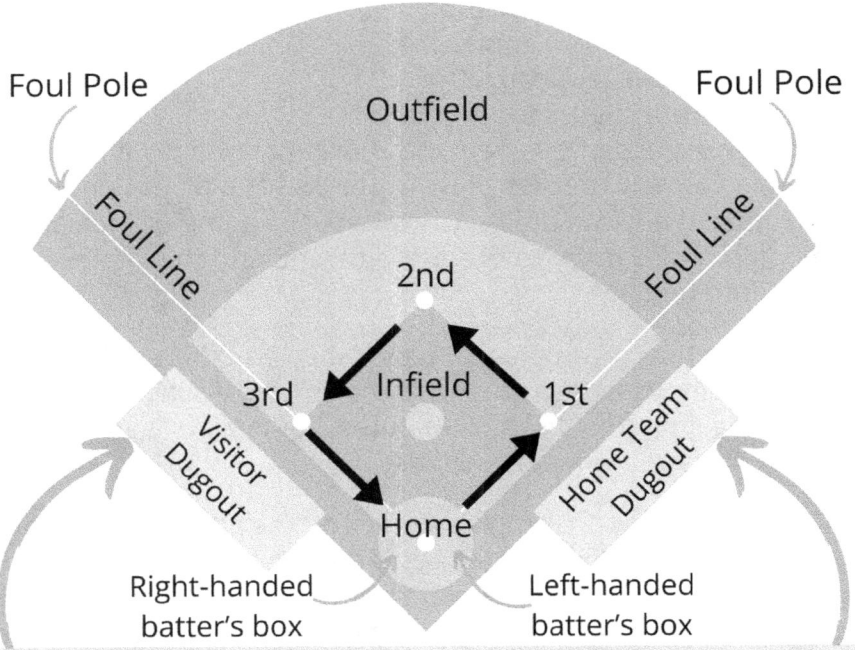

Whose dugout is whose? In the MLB, the home team is usually along the first base line and the away team is along the third base line. In youth baseball, more influential factors are which team gets there first and chooses the one with better shade. If your soon-to-be opponent just finished a game at the same field, they'll stay where they are and your team will go to the other side.

Game time is a loose term - it will set a time limit on when a final regular inning can start, but not on how long it goes. Regardless of time, once an inning starts it will be finished, except in unusual circumstances like deteriorating weather.

Most youth baseball games with players over the age of 9 or 10 average four to five innings. Games with slow innings, or games with younger players, may have three innings. Those with fast innings and/or older players may have up to six or seven, with the maximum number of innings established by the league or tournament. Seven innings is typically the maximum until high school or college, unless a game is tied and there must be a winner, such as in tournament bracket play. If there's a tie at the end of an inning after the game time has expired, the game will usually go to modified rules to try to break the tie and end the game, which we'll go into below.

Let's look at how a game could play out given different variables. For this example, let's say there's a maximum of six innings and a game "time limit" of 1 hour 45 minutes. Some ways a game could end with those parameters include:

- If the teams are both very efficient, the game could be over in an hour and 15 minutes if they complete six innings in that time. They won't start a seventh inning, even though there is extra time, because they've reached the maximum inning limit. Unless there's a tie and the game needs a winner.

- Or maybe the first three innings are pretty slow, and they start a fourth inning at the one hour and 40-minute mark. The umpire will announce when game time has expired and state that they will finish the inning.

- If the home team is ahead, and the away team does not score enough runs in the top of the inning to tie or pull ahead, the game will end at the halfway point of that inning, as soon as the home team gets three outs on the away team. The home team won't hit again in the bottom of the inning because they're already winning and time is up. Similarly, if game time expires while the home team is batting and they're already ahead, the ump may end the game abruptly regardless of the number of outs since there's already a winner.

- If the score is tied or the home team is losing after the top of the inning, they will play into the bottom of the inning. The game will end when:

  - the away team remains ahead, gets three outs, and wins, or

  - the away team gets three outs and the game ends in a tie (if rules for the game/tournament allow that game to end in a tie), or

  - the home team scores enough runs to win. The away team does not need to get three outs to end the inning/game. As soon as the home team pulls ahead in runs, the game will end and the home team will win. This is called a **walk-off**.

- If the score is tied at the end of the inning, and the game can't end in a tie, an extra inning will start with hurry-up-and-break-this-tie modifications. There are variations of these 'overtime' rules, but often each team starts their offensive turn **with a runner already on second base** (usually whoever was their most recent out) and possibly also **one out** counted against them (so the opposing team only needs to get two). Rinse and repeat until somebody wins.

Beware the Eternal Inning

It was a lovely summer evening. The sun had set in a blaze of fiery glory, and the eight-year-olds on the field were feeling quite grown up playing under the phosphorescent buzz of the lights. The air was warm, and we sat among friends watching the kids play. Game time expired, and the umpire announced we would finish the inning. We were the home team and it was the top of the inning. We were down 0 - 783, or thereabouts. We were going to lose this game. Bless our kids' hearts, but we could not get an out. There were passed balls and wild pitches and overthrows galore. It was getting later. Walks and steals and walks and steals. It was getting later. Scoring, scoring, scoring by the other team. It was quite late at this point, and, by rule, this game was not going to end because, as the home team, we were entitled to hit again at the bottom of this inning. Which would begin just as soon as we got three outs. We were never. going. to. get. three. outs. Our coach thought there was hope and wanted to keep trying. Eventually, the opposing coach voluntarily ended their team's at bat (God bless him), so we went to the bottom of the inning. Our team got our chance to hit, and hit we did not. The other team got three quick outs and the game finally, mercifully, ended. Were it not for the grace of the opposing coach, we might still be there today, four years later. I think of him from time to time and wish blessings upon his good, kind soul.

Structure by Age

There are different rules for kids at different ages, helping them learn and develop basic skills in a game that can be very nuanced and situational. As they grow, the game gets bigger: the distance between bases increases incrementally from 60 to 90 feet, the distance from the pitcher's mound to home plate increases from 30 feet to about 60 feet, and game times and the maximum number of innings increase. The details may vary a bit by league and location, but a general overview is included here.

Tee-Ball / Coach Pitch

- Age range = 4-7

- As described in Chapter 1, some leagues may separate Tee-Ball and Coach Pitch; some combine them.

    ◦ For leagues that combine them, an at bat could look like this: a player may get three pitches from their coach. If they don't get a hit, they may get two chances to hit off of a tee. If they don't get a hit off the tee, they strike out.

- Hit balls are played defensively by the opposing team.

- A half inning ends when there are three outs, or possibly when the batting team scores five runs. **Some leagues institute a run maximum for the first three innings** - or maybe for the whole game in tee-ball - to keep one team from running away with the game and allow players on both teams a chance to hit.

- There are no walks, and neither leading off while baserunning nor stealing bases is permitted. **Leading off** means risking a head start by stepping away from the safety of the base they occupy to shorten the run to the next base.

Machine Pitch

- Age range = 7-9

- Coach runs a pitching machine for his own team - often up to four "pitches" per kid

- If a player does not hit any of the pitches, they strike out.

- Hit balls are played defensively by the opposing team.

- An inning ends when there are three outs, or, like in

tee-ball, possibly when one team scores five runs.

- There are no walks and, like in tee-ball, neither leading off nor stealing bases is permitted.

Young Player Pitch

- Age range = starting at 8-10 years old

- The pitcher is a player on the opposing team.

- Strikes, balls, and outs follow typical baseball rules, which are covered later in this chapter.

- In rec leagues at least, there are typically some modified baserunning rules until 11U or 12U, including not allowing leadoffs (see tee-ball section) for baserunners. However, runners may be allowed to start stealing bases with some limitations. Perhaps they can't leave the base they're on until the ball has been pitched and crossed home plate. But, they may be allowed to steal if a "live ball" (at this age, one that hasn't been returned to the pitcher yet) is overthrown and not caught by its target. For example, if the catcher is trying to throw the ball back to the pitcher after a ball or strike (but not a walk), or to the second or third baseman to try to stop a steal, and the receiving player doesn't catch it, baserunners can take advantage of it and keep running.

> **The "8-, 10-, 15-run rule" aka - The Mercy Rule**
>
> This is a way to end a game fairly and consistently when it is lopsided - when one team is crushing the other and the losing team is struggling to get outs.
>
> Rules vary from league to league, but often if one team is ahead by 20 after two innings, 15 after three innings, 10 after four innings, or eight after five innings, the game will end.
>
> Usage example: "We got run ruled." = We lost badly.

- There may still be a run limit for the first few innings (maybe up to 5 runs per team for the first three innings;

unlimited runs starting in the 4th inning) - up to age 10ish.

- Other than maybe 8U, young player pitch teams in competitive tournaments usually just jump into the deep end of the pool and play straight baseball, without the limitations on leadoffs, stealing, or run limits described above.

- Brace yourself. There are (a lot of) wild pitches and passed balls as pitchers and catchers are developing. Most runs in 8U-11U at any level are scored off of walks, passed balls, wild pitches, and stolen bases. We'll go more into each of those mistakes later in the chapter. It can be a little hard to watch, but have faith that they'll get better with practice.

Older Player Pitch

- Age range = by 12U to 14U, if not earlier

- Most of the remaining guardrails come off

- There are still some minor differences between this age and high school/college, but for the most part it's starting to look like real baseball.

Offensive Objective

When it's your team's turn to hit, the objective is to get the bats going and score runs. More runs than the other team. At the end of the day, the goal is to hit the ball hard and fair (= not foul), get on base, avoid outs, and get back home.

Two hurdles must be cleared to earn runs.

Hurdle #1: the pitcher

- The batter needs to get past the pitcher to get on base. They can do this by hitting, getting walked (more on this below), or getting hit-by-pitch (way to wear it!).

- On average, expect about 1 in 3 batters to get on base.*

Hurdle #2: finish getting around the bases to home

- Runners itch to keep going forward. They can run after a teammate's hit. They can also try to steal.

- On average, about 1 in 3 baserunners makes it around to score without 1) getting tagged out themselves, or 2) getting stranded on base when their team gets three outs.*

*Of course, both of these averages are just averages, and will vary - wildly - depending on individual players and how the winds of fortune are blowing during any particular game. They're just included here to illustrate that both getting on base and scoring are beating-the-odds accomplishments! The adage "baseball is a game of failure" comes from the greater likelihood of being put out than scoring.

A **run** is scored by safely rounding/touching all of the bases in order then touching home plate. Touching a base can happen with feet while walking or running, or by sliding/diving to it with their feet or hands. It usually takes a series of plays by multiple batters to round all the bases and score a run, though it can happen all at once with a home run. A **home run** can happen when a ball is crushed / nuked / tatered and goes over the outfield fence between the foul poles, or if the runner is just faster than the fielding and able to get home before the defense can get the ball there. The latter happens most often in younger years, usually due to a train wreck of errors and overthrows in the defending team's haste to make the play. Benefitting from errors means it's not *technically* a home run, but the team will celebrate like it is!

To put a ball in play, the batter needs to hit it between the foul lines. Typically, a batter wants to hit well enough to have time to run to at least first base, or further if possible, before the ball is fielded by the opposing team. Getting the bat on the ball will result in a line drive, a fly ball, a grounder, or a bunt. A **line drive** is a hard, fast, straight hit that lasers the ball past the infielders and out into the outfield grass. This is the hardest kind of hit to field, which lowers the likelihood of an out on the play and increases the odds of that batter getting on base. A **fly ball** - one that flies higher in the air - can be good or bad. If it's a hard, well-placed hit that gets behind or between the outfielders, the batter will likely get to at least second base, or further. Home runs are fly balls that go over the outfield fence. Fly balls to the outfield can also be unlucky if an outfielder can get under it for the catch. **Pop flies**, which go straight up and come down in the infield or just beyond it, are not good because they're usually pretty easy to catch for an easy out. A **grounder** is a hit with little altitude that bounces or rolls on the ground before it's fielded. If it's not hard and fast enough, it will probably get scooped up by an infielder and put quickly into play. A **bunt** is a mini little hit, intentionally bumping the ball directly into the dirt just in front of home plate. Unless the bunter is extremely fast, they often won't make it to base themselves but hope to advance the runners ahead of them - see the section on sacrifices below. The likelihood of any hit being fielded cleanly and quickly for an out increases with the age of the team, and it's fun to watch the kids develop and improve over time.

Foul vs Fair Balls

- A fair ball is in bounds and playable. Runners can advance and the defending team can make plays to get outs.
- A foul ball is out of bounds and "dead". Play is stopped until the next pitch.
- A ball is foul if:
  - it flies out anywhere along the foul line between home plate and either outfield foul pole before hitting the ground and before being touched by a defending player.
  - it lands in fair territory but rolls or bounces over the foul line before/infield of 1st or 3rd base before it's touched by a defender.
- A ball that hits the ground in fair territory and bounces or rolls foul beyond/outfield of 1st or 3rd base remains fair.
- The first two foul balls a batter hits are counted as strikes. Third and additional foul balls do not affect the ball-strike count, but they do increase the pitcher's total pitch count.
- If a defender is able to catch a foul ball before it hits the ground, it is an out.

Sometimes a batter's objective - set by their coach - is to advance the runners ahead of them, rather than to get on base themselves. In these situations - often a **bunt** or short hit - it's considered a **sacrifice** when the batter is out on the play but other runners advance due to that play. There can also be a **sacrifice fly**, when the batter is out due to their fly ball being caught but another runner is able to score. This kind of play can only lead to a score if it's not the third out. **Any runs crossing home plate during a play that results in the third out don't count.**

> ### Dead Ball
>
> A "**dead ball**" is not playable and essentially functions as a time out. Balls die when they're hit foul and not caught, hit fair but out of the park or playable area, when a pitch hits a batter, when a pitcher balks (this mistake is defined in the pitcher position description), when anyone calls "time", and in a variety of interference calls or whenever the umpire says so. When the umpire resumes the game, the ball is returned to the pitcher and the ball is alive again. Hallelujah.

To swing or not to swing. If a pitch is judged by the batter to be unhittable, or outside of the strike zone (defined below), they will (probably) not swing at it. So long as the umpire agrees that it was outside of the strike zone, they will call the pitch a **ball**. So, a ball is both the spherical object being thrown around, as well as a pitch that is judged outside of the strike zone. If there are four balls in a plate appearance, the batter earns a **walk**, which means they get to go to first base without getting a hit. If there is already a runner on first, they will also advance one base, as well as anyone else ahead of them. However, if there is not a **force** (meaning, another runner on base doesn't have to move forward to create space for the guy who just got walked), other runners stay where they are. For example, if there is only a runner on second base when there is a walk, that runner stays there when the walker goes to first. However, if the bases are loaded when there is a walk, the batting team will score a run, since all the runners advance one base to make room for the walker, including the runner on third being forced to home.

When would a player think about not swinging to try to walk? There's possible reward in a free base, but also risk. It is better to earn a walk and get to first base than to strike out swinging at junk. But, it's better to swing at a borderline ball and miss, so at least the batter tried to get a hit, than to **strike out looking**: when an umpire calls a 3rd strike and the batter did not swing, but rather

Count

The **count** is how many balls and strikes have been called during a plate appearance. The first number is balls and the second number is strikes.

When the umpire holds up fingers to indicate the count, the number of balls are on the left hand and strikes on the right.

A **full count** is 3-2 = three balls and two strikes. It's "full" because, unless the batter hits a foul ball, something will happen to end this plate appearance. This batter will: hit to put the ball in play, get a third strike to strikeout, or get a fourth ball and walk to first base.

Image reprinted with written permission from "Referee" Magazine. For subscription information, contact "Referee" magazine at 800-733-6100 or visit referee.com.

just "looked" at it as it went by. Embarrassing. This is one of those situational things, and the decision to swing or not is dependent on other moving parts. What is the count? If it's 3-0 (three balls - no strikes), unless a big juicy meatball screaming "hit me" comes right down Broadway for the fourth pitch, it's probably worth risking a strike to possibly get a fourth ball and walk, especially if the pitcher is throwing a lot of balls. However, if the count is in the pitcher's favor, something like 1-2 (one ball - two strikes), this batter is not close to walking and does not have a cushion of extra strikes, so they'd better swing if it's close. How many outs are there? Are there other runners on base to consider? Coaches will weigh in to direct their players based on their read of the situation.

Batting Order

The **batting order** is the sequence in which players will hit. The **lineup** is the written document identifying both the batting order and which player is assigned to which defensive position. While players may change defensive positions during a game, they are required to hit in the same order for the whole game unless they're substituted by a player from the bench. Once a player has been swapped out of the lineup, the coaches will notify the umpire and the opposing team to avoid confusion.

The number of players allowed on the lineup changes as players and teams mature. At younger ages, all the players will be in the lineup so they all can hit. Later on, coaches may be limited by rules to only nine or 10 players in a lineup for a game.

How do coaches decide on the batting order? At younger ages, coaches will likely mix up the order from game to game to give all the kids a chance to hit in the top of the line up. As kids get older and teams get more competitive, the lineup order becomes more strategic and performance-based. The players who hit and get on base most consistently will be in the top half of the lineup. The top of the lineup is likely to get more chances to hit than the bottom of the lineup, so having strong hitters there increases the likelihood of hits and runs. Stacking strong hitters one after the other also increases the likelihood of getting players on base and around to score. While each coach is their own kind of artist in determining the batting order based on their players' record, recent performance, and potential, there are some general strategies about who to consider putting where and why.

Batter 1: The Leadoff Hitter. This batter's performance sets the initial tone - of excitement and hope, or disappointment - and gets things rolling strategically for the batters behind them. So, coaches want this to be someone who consistently gets on base, whether by hit or by walk or by whatever. Just get on base. It's also helpful if they're speedy and good at stealing bases, so they're ready to run home with a little help from a batter behind them.

> You are now entering a shallow rabbit hole about **batting out of order**. If a player accidentally (or intentionally) bats out of order, and the opposing team calls them on it **before a pitch is thrown to the next legal batter**, some drama may ensue.
>
> 1) The person who should have batted, not the one who actually batted, will be called out, and
>
> 2) anything that happened as a result of the illegal batter is erased and rewound.
>
> But, if the defending team appeals an improper batter **after** a pitch has been thrown to the following batter, they've missed the boat. It's too late to appeal. There is no penalty, and play continues as normal, picking up at the spot in the batting order following the improper-but-now-legal batter.

Batter 2: This should also be a consistent hitter who can help to advance the leadoff hitter, and ideally get on base themselves. You don't want someone who frequently hits into a double play (defined more extensively in the defense section; in short, a play for two outs), as that would erase any progress of the leadoff and get the team in trouble on outs going into the meat of the lineup.

Batter 3: The 3 hole. This is often the best hitter, with both a high batting average and on-base percentage. This spot balances the benefit of (possibly) more at bats than the 4th and later batters, while hopefully having runners ahead of them to send home.

Batter 4: The Cleanup. This is usually the best power hitter, and the goal is for them to get RBIs by driving forward any of the first three batters left on base. Due to their spot, they have the best chance of coming up to bat with the bases loaded.

Batter 5: This is a batter who hits for extra bases and doesn't strike out often, who can bring home anyone left on base.

Batter 6: Usually also a good hitter, but perhaps not as consistent as the batters ahead of them. They may also be a good base runner, to create opportunities for runs in the bottom of the lineup.

Batters 7-9+: Unless you're on a lucky team full of players with a great batting average, the less-consistent hitters usually go in the bottom of the lineup, with progressively lower performance as you go further down. However, depending on the coach's strategy, there could be strong hitters sprinkled throughout the lineup. Or, the last hitter may be a good hitter to try to flip back to the top of the lineup and/or a speedy runner who, if they can get on base, will be available to score when the top of the lineup starts again. The bottom of the lineup can be a good spot for players who are still learning the game and developing their swing and confidence, as they will likely have fewer at bats than the top of the lineup.

Basic Batting Statistics

Let's begin to define the alphabet soup of baseball statistics, with a focus here on those related to trying to score runs. Additional stat definitions are included in the defense section with their relevant position descriptions.

Keeping and analyzing player data is a baseball tradition. Noting balls, strikes, hits, runs, and errors on a scoresheet can be a fun way to feel connected to and better follow along with a game.

But there's a lot of letters here, and even if we know what they mean and how they're calculated, what are "good" statistics? This will change as players grow and develop. While a player, their teammates, and their opponents are still learning the game and developing their skills, statistics are (a lot) less meaningful. I've included what's considered "good" at the high school level for a few stats as a point of reference. But again, **a lot of stats are skewed (a lot) in younger players and should be consumed heavily salted for many reasons**: there's a small sample size (few games), influence from the quality (or not) of opposing pitchers, differing rules, a smaller field size, and more. And of course, any statistics, even skewed, are only as good as the scorekeeper who records them. With many youth baseball scorekeepers new to the job and/or struggling to keep up, bad data is a likely confounding factor, as well.

Frankly, stats can continue to be a bit subjective in high school, college, and beyond, dependent on judgement calls by the scorekeeper. If a scorekeeper is stricter on what they'll call a hit (vs. a 'reached on error' – see below), a player's batting average will be lower. And all of their other statistics that factor in the batting average are affected by those judgement calls, too.

All that said, let's dive in.

PA = Plate appearances = total # times it was a player's turn in the batting order, regardless of the result

AB = At bat = subset of PAs

- Things that count as an at bat:
  ~ Hits
  ~ Reaching base by fielder's choice (see below)
  ~ Reaching base due to an error by the defense
  ~ Getting called out for any reason <u>other</u> than a sacrifice bunt or fly; so, striking out or being fielded out would be an AB

- Things that <u>do not count</u> as an at bat:
  ~ Getting a free base due to walking, hit by pitch, or an interference call on the defense (usually catcher interference)
  ~ Sacrifice bunt or fly

H = Hits = a hit is only technically a hit if 1) the batter gets safely to a base, 2) nobody else on their team gets out as a result of their hit, and 3) the opposing team fields the hit (relatively) cleanly. However, especially for younger players, the game scorekeeper may play in the gray area here and count as hits what would be a FC or ROE (see below) for older kids. A routine out at first is different in 8U than in 14U; meaning, play should be cleaner at older ages.

- **FC = Fielder's Choice** = If the batter 'hits' the ball and they get safely to a base, but the defending team tags out a runner ahead of them, it's counted as a "fielder's choice", not a hit. Meaning, the opposing team had their choice of who to get out, because the ball wasn't hit hard/far enough for everyone to stay safe.

- **ROE = Reached on Error** = If the batter makes it safely to a base only because the defending team made one or more errors fielding. Meaning, the runner would have been out if the defending team had executed what should be a routine play. A common example of this in youth baseball is missing the out at first due to the throw there being wild, or the 1st baseman not catching a catchable throw. But where, *exactly*, is the line between a "routine" play and an error? That's where the scorekeeper judgement comes in, coloring the hits statistic and others that trickle down from it.

- Four types of hits:
  ~ **1B = Single** = batter makes it safely to first base
  ~ **2B = Double** = batter makes it safely to second base
  ~ **3B = Triple** = batter makes it safely to third base
  ~ **HR = Home run!** = batter makes it safely around all the bases and back home on the hit

AVG = Batting Average = # hits / # at bats

- A good batting average in high school is 0.300 or better. After high school, having a batting average that high gets harder, and being in the 300's is even more impressive.

RBI = Runs Batted In = # runs scored due to a batter's plate appearance. RBIs are usually due to hits that advance the runners, but are also earned if bases are loaded when a batter is walked or hit by pitch, forcing the runner at third base to home for a run. Batters can also earn an RBI for a run earned on a sacrifice fly, as long as it's not part of a double play. RBIs are not credited to the batter if a run is earned due to a fielding error.

R = Runs = # times a player crosses home plate themselves to earn a run

BB = Base on Balls (walks) = # times a player advances to first base due to a pitcher throwing four balls during their plate appearance

OBP = On-Base Percentage = It sure is easier to score once you've cleared the hurdle of getting on base, so OBP can be a good indicator of productiveness for the team in scoring. There's a little bit of weird math to get to the number. (Hits + Walks + Hit by Pitch) / (At Bats + Walks + Hit by Pitch + Sacrifice Flies). While a player technically gets on base with a ROE or FC, they are not counted as getting on base for the sake of this statistic, since getting there wasn't clean.

- A good OBP in high school is 0.500-0.600 or more.

SLG = Slugging Percentage = This measures what it kind of sounds like: hitting power. It's like a batting average that weights hits that earn more bases. (1B + 2Bx2 + 3Bx3 + HRx4)/AB or, more simply, (total bases earned by hits)/AB

- A good SLG in high school is 0.500 or more.

OPS = On-Base Percentage Plus Slugging = This is meant to show how complete a player's hitting skills are, combining how consistently a player gets on base with their hitting power. OBP + SLG

- A good OPS in high school is 0.800 or more.

SO = Strikeouts = # of times a player is out due to three strikes during an at bat

K-L = Strikeouts Looking = subset of SO; # of times a player strikes out by watching the ball go by rather than trying to take a swing at it. Face-palm statistic.

HBP = Hit by pitch = # of times a player advances to first base due to getting beaned by the pitcher. Statistic measuring how often a player took one for the team, and/or how unlucky they are. Also measures contribution to team bruise contest.

SAC or SH = Sacrifice Hits & Bunts = # times a ball is intentionally hit short by the batter to advance a runner at the cost of getting out themselves

SF = Sacrifice Fly = # times a fly ball is hit into the outfield or foul territory that is caught for an out but allows a runner to score. This only works if a team has less than two outs before the at-bat, because a fly ball caught for a third out would prevent any runners from scoring.

SB = Stolen Bases = # of bases a runner advances at a time other than immediately following a hit. This thievery can happen while a pitcher is throwing a pitch, if a wild pitch or passed ball gets behind the catcher, or even while the pitcher or catcher has the ball in hand, if the runner (or their 3rd base coach, who is likely calling the shots here) is feeling lucky. In younger leagues, base stealing may not be allowed, or may be limited.

SB% = Stolen Base Percentage = # bases stolen / # of attempts

CS = Caught Stealing = # times out as a runner due to unsuccessful base stealing

PIK or PK = Picked Off = # times out as a runner due to the pitcher or catcher finding them too far off base between pitches. The pitcher or catcher throws the ball to a fielder who tags the errant runner (picks them off) before they can run, dive, or slide back to their base.

Defensive Objective

When a team is playing defense - pitching and fielding - their goal is to prevent the opposing team from earning runs. They want to get three outs as fast as possible to end the half inning and return to batting. A perfect defense is a 1-2-3 inning, meaning that the defending team gets an out on each of the first three batters they face. This obviously keeps the opposing team from scoring. It also preserves the pitcher. The more pitches a pitcher throws for each batter, and cumulatively in each inning, the sooner they will need to be swapped out for a fresh pitcher, either by rule due to a high pitch count and/or fatigue. A team wants to keep a strong pitcher on the mound as long as they can and not wear them out early.

Common Outs

Strikeouts - When a batter accumulates three strikes, they are out. Strikes happen when:

- a pitcher throws a pitch in the **strike zone** that isn't hit, whether the batter swings and misses or watches it go by

- a batter **swings and misses** at any pitch, whether or not it was in the strike zone. This includes a checked swing that... isn't checked on time. If a batter starts to swing the bat but stops, it's called a **checked swing**. But, if the bat comes too far around, even if they don't fully swing, it can be a strike - this call is up to the umpire.

  - If you hear someone say, "Oh, yes he did!" without further context, they're often referring to whether a batter swung the bat enough for it to be called a strike.

- a batter hits **foul balls**. However, fouls will only count towards the first two strikes - you can't get a third strike from a foul ball. So, once there are two strikes, there's really no limit on how many foul balls a batter can hit.

Strike Zone

- The **strike zone** is the block of space above home plate between the batter's mid-torso and knees. The vertical dimensions of the strike zone will vary depending upon the height of the batter.
- Umpires usually allow for a larger strike zone when kids first start pitching. This helps new pitchers who are still learning and developing, and encourages batters to swing rather than waiting to be walked. The strike zone shrinks as kids grow and pitches (usually) become more accurate.
- Where the batter is standing in the box does not matter - the strike zone remains in the same place over the plate.

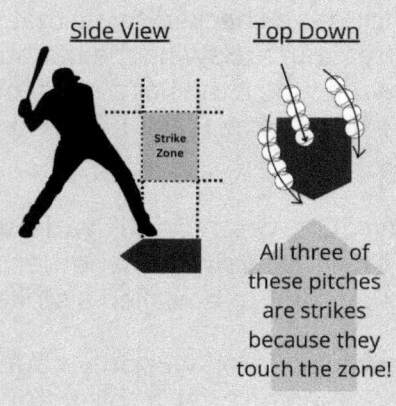

Side View   Top Down

Strike Zone

All three of these pitches are strikes because they touch the zone!

A batter starts to look like they're a survivor despite the odds after hitting three, four, or more fouls in an at bat, earning "Way to stay alive!" cheers from their section. While they may or may not ultimately get a hit or get on base, fouling off a bunch of balls increases the pitcher's pitch count, tiring them out faster and possibly speeding their departure from the game. An at bat with eight or more pitches is considered a "**Quality At Bat**" (QAB) for the batter even if they don't get a hit.

Catches - When any defending player **catches a hit ball before it touches the ground**. This catch can be anywhere on the field, including in foul territory.

Force outs - When a fielder holding the ball beats a runner to a base when that runner was required - or 'forced' - to advance to that base. This happens most routinely at first base. When a batter hits the ball, they're required to run to first base. If the defending team fields it quickly and beats them there, the batter/runner is out. But a force out can happen at any base. Runners are 'forced' forward to the next base if there is another runner coming from the prior base. There can only be one runner on a base at a time. If the runner on a base does not go forward, the runner behind them can be trapped between occupied bases and tagged out.

Tag outs - When a fielder with the ball in their glove tags a runner with their glove, or with the ball itself, anytime a runner is not touching a base. If a runner is touching a base, they're safe. If they're off of the base in any variety of circumstances (running, actively stealing, leading off between pitches, standing around not paying attention, etc.), they're fair game to tag out.

Less-Common Outs

Baserunner interference - If a baserunner interferes with a fielder making a play, like bumping into them or blocking a catch, etc.

Batter interference - Any movement by a batter that interferes with a catcher's ability to make a play, by blocking their sightline or their ability to throw out or tag a runner stealing any base, including home plate.

Failure to tag up after a catch - This one's a little weirder. After the fielding team catches a flyball (or a line drive, if they're brave and lucky) for an out, a runner can try to steal the next base. But, they have a job to do first. After the catch is made, the runner has to go back and touch the base they were on (the base they were leading off/away from) before they can try to steal the next one. If they don't go back and tag up, they can't legally occupy the next base, so they're out.

Illegal base running / running outside of the baseline - This one's also a little wonky. Technically, there is no such thing as a

A **pickle** is tart, salty, and always exciting! This is when a runner gets trapped between bases. You'll see them running back and forth between the base they left and the next one while the defending team throws the ball back and forth trying to tag them out. A runner gets into this situation when they try to steal or advance on a run, but the defending team gets the ball to their intended base before the runner. If it's not a force, the runner could be safe at either base, so the defending team needs to actually tag them with the ball to get them out. It's a race. Who will win?! Break out the popcorn!

base path. As long as a runner doesn't walk off the field or otherwise abandon any effort to remain in the game and reach the next base, a runner can kind of go wherever they want, though it's risky to wander too far from the safety of a base. This changes once the fielding team attempts to tag that runner. At the moment of the attempted tag, a virtual line is drawn between the runner and the base they're attempting to reach, and the runner cannot veer more than three feet on either side of that line to avoid a tag. If they do dodge outside of that new and temporary base path, they're out. This avoids the situation of a fielder chasing a runner all over the place trying to tag them out. If there are multiple tag-out attempts on a play (like in a pickle), the base path resets between the runner's new position and the desired base each time a tag is attempted.

A runner can also potentially be out if they cause interference when they're running toward first base. There is a 'running lane' in the last half of the distance between home and first which is three feet to the right of the foul line. If the batter/runner veers outside of this lane and gets in the way of a routine throw that the first baseman is not able to catch, the batter/runner is out.

Pitching Efficiency + Fielding Efficiency = Game Flow

As mentioned earlier, depending upon the performance of the pitcher and the rest of the fielders, innings can be fast or slow. The fastest possible half inning would be three pitches, and it requires perfect over-the-plate pitching + batters who hit + perfect fielding. Perhaps Batter 1 swings and pops up a fly ball that's caught by the shortstop, Batter 2 hits a ground ball to the second baseman who throws it to first base for the out, and Batter 3 hits a long fly ball that's caught by the center fielder. Three pitches. Three outs. Half inning over. Go put your batting gloves back on, team.

An "Immaculate Inning" is nine pitches for nine consecutive strikes = three outs. This rare kind of inning is won by the pitcher on their own and is a badge of honor for them.

What's some extra exciting fielding? Getting more than one out on a play. A **Double Play** is when there are two outs on the same play. A **Triple Play** is getting all three outs on one play. Now that's efficiency.

While multiple outs on a play can happen in a variety of situations, one of the most common double plays is layering two force outs. For example, let's say there's a runner on first base and their teammate hits a grounder that's scooped up by the shortstop. The shortstop throws it to the second baseman, who gets out #1 when they step on second base, assuming they beat the runner coming from first who's being forced to second by the hit. Then the second baseman throws it to first base for out #2, if the first baseman catches it and touches the base before the batter/runner arrives. A triple play could add on a third force out if there were two or three runners on base before the hit. Caught pop flies and a tag outs are also common elements of multiple-out plays. Fielding needs to be clean and fast to execute a double or triple play, and it's super fun to watch, especially when a team does it for the first time.

There can also be - and more often are - slow innings. The batting team could be hitting and scoring a lot, going deep into or maybe even repeating their line-up. Or, the pitcher could be throwing a bunch of balls for walks. Or fielders could be making errors and missing outs. Or, the batting team may not be hitting or scoring much but still wears down the pitcher with a bunch of fouls and long at bats.

Umpire Hand Signals

When making calls, umpires may use their voice, but they always use a hand signal. Included here are some of the most common signals.

Safe
Umpires will sweep both of their hands from the center out to the sides if a runner is safe.

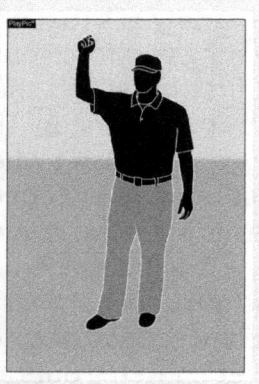

Out
Umpires will hold up a fist if a player is out.

Foul Ball or Time
When a ball is hit foul, or if anyone calls time, or if the ball dies for another reason, the umpire will hold up both hands to stop play. They may hold up one hand for a short pause in pitching.

Play

The umpire will point at the pitcher and say "play" whenever they're ready to start or resume play. This could be at the beginning of an inning, or to get things rolling again after a foul or time out.

What about balls and strikes, you say?

Umpires get a little creative on this point. For balls, they may gesture their hand up, down, or sideways to indicate where the ball missed the zone. But just as often, they don't make any signal or say anything at all for a ball. For strikes, they will verbally say "Strike!" or "Hah!" and may point to the side with one or two fingers, indicating if it was a first or second strike. Sometimes they'll raise their fist for a strike (like they do for an out), but more often they point to the side. Sometimes they'll point at the batter if the strike was due to a swing and miss. On the third strike they'll call a strike and point to the side, and also raise their fist for an out, as shown above. Some awesome umps really get into calling strikes, with a whole whooping, pointing, punching routine that's a fun little show. :)

All umpire PlayPics reprinted with written permission from "Referee" Magazine. For subscription information, contact "Referee" magazine at 800-733-6100 or visit referee.com.

Depending on the rules and the situation, coaches may choose to pull a pitcher before they reach a certain pitch count. This could be due to their performance, mindset, and/or maybe they're doing fine but the coach wants them to be able to throw again in another game that afternoon or the following day. Since pitching has a limit, coaches will be strategic on how and when to spend the pitches available from their different players. Long innings, like those described above, may throw a wrench in their original plans.

Leagues and tournaments put a cap on the number of pitches and/or innings a pitcher can throw per day or per tournament for the safety and arm health of young pitchers. In addition, there may be required days of rest that increase incrementally with the number of pitches thrown. We'll dig in more on this below.

Positions

Each of the kids standing around on the field have a different job during the game. We'll go through each role, why it's important, and skills or attributes that can be helpful to a player in that position.

Positions by Number

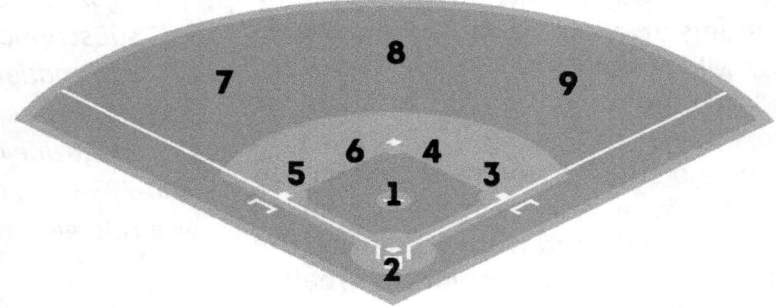

Pitcher (RHP or LHP)

Position #1

- RHP = right-handed pitcher

- LHP = left-handed pitcher

Primary job: Throw the ball from the pitcher's mound to the catcher through the strike zone, or close enough to it to bait a batter into swinging. The pitcher wants to get a batter out due to strikes, or for hits to be weak and easily fielded by their teammates.

Secondary jobs:

- Pick off runners who are off their base. If a runner is leading too far off their base in anticipation of the pitch, and the pitcher can laser the ball to a nearby teammate fast enough, they can tag the runner out before they run or dive back to the base. Or, if the runner decides to go for it and begins the steal attempt, the pitcher can throw it to the fielder at the next base to tag the runner out before they arrive.

- Field a ball if it's hit near the pitcher's mound

- Cover home if the catcher is scrambling to retrieve a ball that got behind them and there's a runner coming in trying to score; the catcher will throw the ball to the pitcher to tag the runner.

- Cover first or third base if those positions leave their base to field a ball

> **Picked Off vs. Caught Stealing**
>
> This is really the difference in where a runner is tagged out between bases. They're picked off if they're tagged out leading off from or otherwise not touching the base they already occupy. They're caught stealing if they're actively running or sliding toward the next base and tagged out before they get there.

Helpful attributes for success:

- Strong arm

- For younger players - the ability to just get the ball consistently over the plate in the strike zone

- For older players - in addition to ball control, the ability to throw hard and to throw several different kinds of pitches, to keep the batter guessing about the next pitch's speed and movement

- Calm demeanor – Pitching is the front-and-center position of the defense, with a lot of the team's success riding on their performance. They need to be able to shrug off mistakes and perform under pressure.

- Left-handed – Most pitchers, like most people, are right-handed. However, left-handed pitches move differently than right-handed ones do, which can throw a batter off. Since left-handed pitchers are rarer, they may be coveted by coaches to add to their pitching arsenal. Lefties also look straight at first base when preparing to pitch (vs. righties, whose back is to first), making it easier to pick off runners leading off there.

Common labels for pitchers:

- **Starter** - the first one up. At higher levels, this may be one of your strongest pitchers, who gets the game off to a good start and may play deep into the game. On younger teams, players will likely take turns in the starting position, or coaches may even put in weaker pitchers early to give them a chance to practice and learn while the game is still young.

- **Reliever** - they come in to relieve the starter, or to relieve another reliever.

- **Closer** - the last pitcher. This is often a stronger pitcher who the coach can count on to get some quick outs to close/end the game quickly to secure a win.

To win a game you must have good pitching. Good pitching means throwing consistently over the plate, and either racking up strikes for strikeouts or allowing hits that the rest of the team can field for outs. If a pitcher is throwing lots of balls and wild pitches, they're in trouble. Lots of balls loads up the bases with walkers (now runners), and enough walks will start forcing in runs. Wild pitches cause stealing frenzies. When the ball gets past the catcher, runners will run and steal as much as they think they can get away with, maybe even scoring, while the catcher scrambles for the ball.

In youth baseball, many/most players on a team will pitch in addition to playing another position. Once they get to high school, some players will start to be **Pitcher Only (PO)**. Since there are limits to how many pitches one kid can throw in a game, and how many innings/games they can play in a tournament, it is helpful for a team to have a "deep **bullpen**" (meaning lots of good pitchers; the "bullpen" is the area where the pitchers warm up). You can expect that, unless your kid is a catcher (and even then sometimes), they will likely pitch at some point.

Common lore is that young players should only throw fast balls (not curve balls or sliders) until they're at least 12 or 13, though they may want to wait longer depending on the individual player's development. Some in the medical community[1] , however, don't believe there's conclusive evidence that throwing curve balls is more dangerous than fast balls, which also stress an arm due to the greater force used to achieve high velocity. As mentioned above, many leagues and tournaments will have maximum pitch counts in place to protect young arms by placing limits on how much they can throw. If you have an aspiring pitcher, **it may be worth investing in a few pitching lessons to ensure good mechanics** in their throwing motion. A coach can make sure they're throwing safely and help improve their performance.

Common pitching stats:

- IP = Innings Pitched

- GP = Games Pitched

- GS = Games Started

- BF = Total Batters Faced

1. https://www.ncbi.nlm.nih.gov/pmc/articles/PMC6874692/

- #P = Total Pitches

- W = Wins = Yay!

- L = Losses = Bah!

- SV = Saves = When a pitcher enters a game when their team is ahead by fewer than three runs, and the win is in jeopardy due to runners already on base and/or upcoming batters, and their performance preserves the lead to win.

- SVO = Save Opportunities

- BS = Blown Saves. Womp womp.

- SV% = Save Percentage

- H = Hits allowed

- R = Runs allowed

- ER = Earned Runs allowed = Runs earned cleanly and only by the actions of the batting team. So, runs earned without the batter/runner benefitting from passed balls or other errors by the defending team.

- BB = Base on Balls (walks)

- SO = Strikeouts

- K-L = Strikeouts Looking = The batters just watched these go by...

- S% = Strike Percentage = ideally greater than 50%

- HBP = Batters Hit By Pitch = Eek! Sorry about that!

- ERA = Earned Run Average = (ER / IP) x maximum number of possible innings in the game for their age

  - A good ERA in high school is between 3.00-4.00. A

pitcher at a D1 college would want an ERA below 2.00.

- WHIP = Walks plus hits per innings pitched

    ○ A good WHIP in high school is 2.00 or less.

- LOB = Runners left on base

- BK = Balks = Whoops. See below for more on this one.

- PIK = Runners Picked Off = Gotcha!

- CS = Runners Caught Stealing = Gotcha, too!

- SB = Stolen Bases allowed = When they make it, dammit.

- SB% = Stolen Bases allowed Percentage

- WP = Wild Pitches = C'mon catcher! Why couldn't you get a glove on the one 10 feet over your head?!

- BAA or OBA = Batting Average Against or Opponent Batting Average = H / (BF - BB - HBP - sacrifice hits or flies - catcher interference)

Common mistakes

- Balls/walks – Some walks are just part of the game. They only really become a problem if additional walks, or wild pitches/base stealing, start to run up the score of the opponent.

- Wild Pitches – When a pitch is so far outside the strike zone that it's difficult or impossible for the catcher to catch it and one or more runners advance.

- Hit by Pitch – When a pitch hits the batter, they get to go to first base and will force forward a runner already on first, and any immediately in front of them.

- Balk – In short, this is illegal movement before a pitch.

There's a lot of nuance here, and this is one of those rules dependent on the judgment of the umpire. Generally, after a pitcher gets set (moving their feet together and raising the ball in front of their chest), any motion must result in a throw. If they don't make a throw and don't step all the way off the mound before getting reset, a balk can be called. At younger ages, or early in the season, or early in an individual game, or when there's a new pitcher, umpires may give warnings before enforcing a balk. But, if it is called, any runners on base advance one. If there's a runner on third, they score. This rule is intended to control a pitcher's movement and prevent them from "faking out" a batter or potential base stealer.

Catcher (C)

Position #2

Primary job: Squat behind home plate, catch or block every pitch, and return it cleanly to the pitcher. They don't ever want a ball to get behind them.

Secondary jobs:

- Signal to pitcher the recommended next pitch, passing along a coach's signal or making their own judgment based on the situation. Get annoyed if the pitcher shakes them off.

- Stick or frame ball after catching it, non-verbally encouraging the umpire to call the pitch a strike

  - Sticking = freezing the glove for a moment right where they caught the ball, illustrating for the umpire where the ball crossed the plate

  - Framing = moving the glove *slightly* further into the strike zone after catching the ball. A touch of framing can help the pitcher by putting some figurative lipstick on the pitch, helping it look more definitively like a strike. Significant framing (grabbing a ball from way up high or outside and moving it in) is... kind of funny. *Yeah, that was a strike, Blue. It was right here!* Ump rolls eyes and calls a ball.

- Prevent stolen bases.

  - During a pitch, a runner may take off from first or second base to steal the next one. If there's time and they're fast enough, the catcher can throw the ball to second or third to try to beat the runner and get them out. While either of these can be a great and important play, there is a risk: if the fielder doesn't (or can't) receive the throw from the catcher, the runner will likely advance even further than the base they were trying to steal, possibly even scoring. Executing this well requires a catcher with a fast and accurate throw and a fielder who is both paying attention and can reliably catch the throw and tag out the runner.

- Field balls that batters pop straight up. They'll usually rip off their helmet before looking up so they can see better.

Helpful attributes for success:

- Strong legs - because all that squatting

- Strong and accurate arm, and a quick **pop time** (the total time from catching a pitched ball to its arrival in the 2nd baseman's glove, including getting up from squatting and throwing across the diamond) – for throwing out wannabe base stealers

- Reliable ball stopper – whether by catching, body blocking, or smothering into the dirt with their glove, you want a catcher who can (at least almost) always keep the ball from getting past them

- Good baseball IQ - always understanding the situation and

having the confidence to quickly direct teammates during a play by calling where the ball should be thrown

Crowds and commentators often focus on the pitcher as the centerpiece of defense, while the guy squatting behind the dish, hidden behind a face mask and other gear, may be overlooked or taken for granted. But the catcher is often a leader on the team. See Crash Davis (Kevin Costner) in *Bull Durham* (this is not a kids' movie, BTW. Whoops...). Or Jake Taylor (Tom Berenger) in *Major League*. Or Dottie Hinson (Geena Davis) in *A League of Their Own*! By the nature of their position, they have a unique perspective on the field, and can help direct action by their teammates in the heat of the moment. They see every pitch and get to know the habits of the opposing batters. They are the umpire's "best friend" (catching balls before they hit them in the face) and may chat them up throughout the game.

When you have a solid catcher, they help keep the game under control. They minimize stolen bases - both by throwing out (or threatening to) anyone trying to steal 2nd or 3rd, and, most importantly, capturing every pitch, whether wild or spot on. If there are any runners on base and a ball gets behind the catcher - as a **passed ball** (PB) or a **wild pitch** (WP) - the wheels can come off and things can get crazy with stolen bases, including home, while the catcher scrambles around for the ball.

The catcher also has a feel for how the pitcher is doing - if they're dialed in, getting tired, or stressed. They may make a visit to the mound to check on them, give them a heads up about an upcoming play, or to tell them a joke or ask what they're getting for lunch after the game if they need them to refocus and calm down.

Catchers throw even more than pitchers in any given game, which is why many coaches won't have their catcher pitch. While their throws are usually not as forceful, unless they're throwing down someone trying to steal 2nd or 3rd base, their throw count is typically higher. For every pitch, the catcher throws it back. And catchers often catch for a whole game, while it's unusual for a single pitcher to pitch a complete game in youth baseball, unless they're incredibly efficient with their outs.

Common Catching Stats

- INN = Innings played as catcher

- PB = Passed balls allowed = Ug. As kids grow, this quickly becomes less and less tolerable.

- SB = Stolen bases allowed = Also ug, but it happens a lot in youth baseball.

- SB-ATT = Stolen bases - stealing attempts

- CS = Runners caught stealing = Gotcha!

- CS% = Runners caught stealing percentage

- PIK = Runners picked off = Gotcha, too!

- CI = Batter advances on catcher's interference = Whoops.

Common Mistakes

- Passed ball – When a catcher fails to catch or block a reasonably placed pitch, and a runner advances or scores while they retrieve the ball.

- Catcher interference – A call by the umpire that the catcher interfered with the batter at any point during a pitch. The batter is awarded first base and all runners forced to advance will advance one. Most often this happens if a catcher reaches forward to receive the pitch and the swinging bat hits their glove.

- Dropped third strike – If the catcher bobbles and drops the ball immediately after a third strike is called, the batter can attempt to run to first base if 1) there isn't someone there already, or 2) there could be someone on first, who would then try to steal as well, but only if there are already two outs. Most of the time they'll still be out, with the catcher retrieving the ball and throwing it to first base before the batter/runner can get there. But sometimes they make it. This rule doesn't usually come online until kids are about 10 or 11 years old.

1st Base (1B)

Position #3

Primary job: Be ready, with a foot on first base, to quickly and cleanly catch a ball fielded by a teammate. On a weak-ish to moderate hit, the team goal is to get the ball to the first baseman before the batter/runner gets there. This is one of the most common plays for an out in baseball.

Baseball Math

See a hat or T-shirt with "6 + 4 + 3 = 2" on it and wonder WTF? It's shorthand for a common double play. The first three numbers refer to the positions playing together and the last number is how many outs. So, shortstop to second base to first base for two outs. Double play.

$$6 + 4 + 3 = 2$$

Secondary jobs:

- Be ready to catch the ball and tag a runner in pickoffs.

- Field any balls hit nearby. Quickly run or throw it to a base, or tag a runner, for an out.

- Act as a cut-off relay for throws from right field to home.

Helpful attributes for success:

- Most important: Has a "good glove," meaning they can reliably catch balls thrown their way. While still helpful to have a good arm, they throw less than other positions.

- Tall - Extra stretch for a ball while keeping a foot on the base can be helpful, though players of any size can be successful at first.

- Left-handed - While there are plenty of right handed first basemen, a leftie's direction of reach can be helpful at the position.

Common errors:

- Not catching a routine ball thrown to them by a teammate

- Not catching a playable ball hit in their direction by a batter

2nd Base (2B)

Position #4

Primary job: Catch/stop/scoop balls hit to the center-right part of the infield and throw it to first. This position, like the shortstop, sees and fields a lot of grounders and line drives. They also catch pop flies landing in their neighborhood.

Secondary jobs:

- Cut-off relay for throws from the outfield

- Cover second base when a runner on first tries to steal

- Backup shortstop for throws to second

Helpful attributes for success:

- Quick reaction time to get a glove on hard-hit balls coming at them like a bullet

- Good baseball IQ and communication - the center infield sees a lot of action so they need to always understand the situation, talk to teammates, and make the right moves for an out without having to stop and think.

- Due to all the action the center infield sees, this player needs to be reliable. A lot of errors in the center infield is a gift to the opposing team. While the second baseman sees a bit less action than the shortstop, on right-handed batters at least, they're still a key element of many infield plays.

Common errors:

- Not catching a playable ball hit in their direction

- Bobbling or dropping a ball

- Throwing wild to a teammate during a play

Shortstop (SS)

Position #6 – So... given common sense... why is this 6 and not 5? Back in the day, shortstop used to play further in the outfield, so its number came after third base. When the modern game brought the shortstop in as part of the infield, they held onto the historic numbering.

Primary job: Catch/stop/scoop balls hit to the center-left part of the infield and throw it to first (or another base, situation-dependent). They are the infield Tasmanian devil - leaping, swooping, and diving for catches that they whip over to a teammate for an out.

> ### Infield Fly Rule
>
> The batter can be called out by the umpire after hitting an infield fly ball, whether the infield catches the fly ball or not.
>
> For this rule to be enforced, it must be easily catchable, and there must be runners on 1st & 2nd or bases loaded.
>
> **This rule is meant to protect runners from an easy double play**, and is not intended just as a free out for the defending team (since the runners aren't forced to advance).

Secondary jobs:

- Shortstop is often the leader of the infield arc, communicating plays and working in close tandem with their wingman, the second baseman.

- They may relay signals for plays like pickoffs to the pitcher, catcher, and others.

- They typically catch throws to second base for an out, and are backed up by the second baseman.

- They may often be involved in starting a double play.

Helpful attributes for success:

- Shortstop is typically filled by one of the most talented and reliable fielders. They need to be athletic with quick reaction time, have great lateral movement, and catch and field the multitude of balls that will be hit their way at high speed.

- Like the second baseman, they need to always be dialed-in to the situation and know where the play is.

- Also like the second baseman, multiple errors at shortstop can mean trouble, due to the amount of action they see in the center infield.

Common errors:

- Not catching a playable ball hit in their direction

- Bobbling or dropping a ball

- Throwing wild to a teammate during a play

3rd Base (3B) - aka "The Hot Corner"

Position #5

Primary job: Catch/stop/scoop balls hit to the left part of the infield and throw it to first (or another base, situation-dependent). Cover third base to receive throws there during plays.

Secondary jobs:

- They also often start double plays, either by stepping on third if there is a forced runner coming, or throwing to second.

- Be ready to catch a ball from the pitcher or catcher for a pick off or to catch someone stealing.

Helpful attributes for success:

- Reliable fielder to get a glove on balls hit or thrown their way. A lot of balls get hit that direction, as they do to the shortstop, due to most hitters being right-handed.

- This position requires more strength than speed. They need a strong and accurate arm to frequently throw fielded balls across the diamond to first base for an out.

- Good baseball IQ - due to the number of hits they field, they should know where the highest-priority out is at all times, and have good reflexes to execute it.

Common errors:

- Not catching a ball hit or thrown in their direction

- Bobbling or dropping a ball

- Throwing wild to a teammate during a play

Outfielders (LF, CF, RF)

Position #7 = Left Field (LF)

Position #8 = Center Field (CF)

Position #9 = Right Field (RF)

Primary job: Catch or quickly retrieve balls hit to the outfield; ideally catching a fly ball before it hits the ground for an out, or at least retrieving it and throwing it to the infield quickly (sometimes via a cut-off) to minimize base running.

Secondary job: Back up overthrows or missed balls from the infield.

Helpful attributes for success:

- Being able to track a ball in the air and anticipate where it will land, and, if they can't get under the ball, make situational judgements on when to dive for it or when to let it bounce

- Speed - there's lots of ground to cover in the outfield. The most athletic or speediest player on the team is often at Center Field, as they cover the most territory.

- Reliable at catching

- Strong throwing arm

- Mental fortitude to always be dialed in and not daydreaming when the game seems far away in the infield

The outfield is often looked at as Timbuktu when baseball players are young. Indeed, until they grow and become stronger hitters, most of the action is in the infield and a lot of daisy picking happens in the outfield. This all changes when players get older; strong outfielders become extremely important. An error in the infield may be a one-base mistake, but an error in the outfield can allow the other team to get two, three, or all four bases on a play.

> **Ground Rule / Automatic Double**
>
> If you see an outfielder hold their hands up in the air, they're not saying that a field goal is good. Wrong game.
>
> They're likely calling 'time' due to a ground rule or automatic double. This happens when a ball is hit out of the playable area, but was not a homerun. A ground rule or automatic double could bounce in the outfield before going over the fence, be stuck in a fence, roll underneath something and be out of reach, land in a pile of snow in an early season game that was agreed to be out of bounds, etc. This rule allows a compromise: giving the batter a double for their good hit, but not a homerun since the fielders aren't able to get to the ball to attempt a play.

Common mistakes/errors:

- Misreading a fly ball's trajectory and not being in the right place to catch it

- Dropping a caught fly ball

Common Infield and Outfield Stats:

- TC = Total chances = # of opportunities to help with or execute an out = PO + A + E

- PO = Put outs = # of times taking the final action that results in an out: catching a hit ball, tagging a player, or putting a foot on the base before a runner gets there

- A = Assists = # of times participated in a play when a teammate executed an out

- E = Errors = # of missed routine catches, bobbles, dropped balls, wild throws, or other whoopsies that allow a batter or runner to advance at least one base or score. Errors delay getting three outs, extend the time the pitcher is on the mound, and can change the momentum of the game in favor of the batting team. No bueno.

- FPCT = Fielding percentage = (PO + A) / TC

  - A good FPCT in high school is 0.850 or better. College or MLB players are often in the mid to high 0.900's, almost always making the play that comes their way. It's important to note that a player's position will affect their FPCT. Positions that see a lot of action and more difficult plays, like the middle infield or 3rd base, will likely have a lower FPCT than a catcher or outfielder.

- DP = # Double Plays participated in = Whoop whoop!!

- TP = # Triple Plays participated in = Whoop whoop whoop!!!

Chapter 3
Gear

O k. Here we go. Hold onto your credit cards. Baseball players need a lot of shit. Used to basketball where kids need shoes and... a ball? Or soccer, with its cleats, shin guards, and... a ball? Welcome to the jungle. Football and hockey parents - if you thought baseball was going to be less of a gear hog, my apologies.

Henceforth - when Grandma, Aunt Susan, or anyone else asks what your kid wants for their birthday / Christmas / Hanukkah / St. Patrick's Day / 4th of July / National Macaroni & Cheese Day, the answer is a gift card to your favorite sporting goods store. Because baseball is hungry, and it always needs more of something.

We'll go through all the context in this chapter, explaining what each item is, how important (or not) it is, and estimated costs for each. **See Chapter 7 for a handy dandy budget worksheet that consolidates this (long) list of items and their estimated costs.** There will be other things players think they need that aren't included here, because sellers are gonna sell. Check with your coach to see how essential it is before investing. You'll be plenty invested already.

Slow the Bleeding

We'll go more into cost mitigation in Chapter 7. For now, know that **the price ranges included here are for new items**. If you can get any baseball gear as a hand-me-down from friends or family with older players, say thank you and be grateful! We've been fortunate to get several pairs of cleats and a treasure trove of bats from friends whose kids had outgrown them. When you're done with stuff, share the love and keep the cycle going! We've passed along gear our kids have outgrown to neighbors with younger kids.

Stuff They Wear

Uniform

~ Required
~ Cost varies from $20 up to $400+, depending on the organization.

Rec team uniforms are relatively low-lift. Your coach will probably bring a box of game jerseys and caps in a variety of sizes - the cost of which was likely covered in your registration fee - to an early-season practice. Your kid will come home with whichever one fits best (or whichever one was left when it was their turn to pick). **Your coach will let you know if there's a preference on colors for the pants ($10-$60), socks ($3-$25), and belt ($3-$15), and you'll pick those up on your own at the local sporting goods store**, to which the league may have given you a coupon for some percentage off your order.

Getting **competitive team uniforms** is a bit more of an event. There will likely be a uniform fitting night or three several months before the season starts. During that you'll go to all the stations - jersey, pants, hat, etc. - to have your player try things on and note their sizes on an order form (accounting for potential growth between the fitting and the season starting, so bring your crystal ball). Then you'll place your order, either on paper or through an app/website. **Keep a copy of what you ordered and an itemized receipt.** Your items will arrive near the start of the season in a properly-labeled neat and complete package... or trickle in inconsistently over several weeks with a handful of things missing. Having that receipt you kept will allow for taking inventory, checking off items as you receive them, and will provide the proof you may need when following up on missing stuff.

Typical items in a competitive uniform package:

- Game jerseys - competitive teams usually have at least two

- Pants - long or knickers (short/knee-length) - your player may be able to decide their preference, or the team may want everyone in the same thing. If they wear knickers, they'll also need team-coordinated socks.

> There should be no gap of visible skin between the top of the sock and bottom of the short pants/knickers. They should overlap, otherwise you end up with "kneevage". Lol. And probably a bandaid.

If they're on a competitive team with more than one jersey, they'll have the same number of pants as jerseys, which will coordinate with a specific top.

- Socks - while these are usually part of the uniform, they only really matter for players wearing knickers, otherwise you can't see them anyway. They may have specific socks to go with specific jerseys, if there's more than one.

> If you're on a team with **multiple uniforms** that each have multiple pieces, figure out how to keep track of:
> 1) which items go together, and
> 2) which jerseys are worn on which day
>
> You could keep your own list, or you could coordinate with other moms using a shared online doc. And/or build uniform notes into the app your team uses to coordinate game/practice schedules.

- Belt - one or more - could be coordinated with a specific jersey

- Cap - one or more - could be coordinated with a specific jersey

- Practice shirts - Some teams want everyone wearing the same practice shirt on the same day; others don't care.

- Hoodie - This may be part of the uniform, but is most often used for warmups or during practice on colder days. And for wearing to school to be cool.

Whatever level your kid is playing, and however the uniform arrives, it's usually a fun day for your player. It's exciting to see what this year's uniforms look like and to try them on (unless they got stuck with a too-big or too-small jersey left at the bottom of the box). It makes the start of the season seem more real!

So, while we know the kids wear these newly acquired uniforms on game days, **what should players wear to practice**? Some coaches or organizations don't care – kids can show up to practice in whatever athletic T-shirt and shorts they may have been wearing already that day. Others have more specific expectations, wanting players in baseball pants and perhaps coordinating shirts (practice shirts are usually just for competitive teams, and not even all of them). **Err on the side of wearing baseball pants to practice at least until you get a feel for your team's culture.** If your coach does want players to wear baseball pants to practice, consider buying some discount ones (or use last season's game pants to practice in, if they still fit), so that current uniform/game pants don't get worn out early in the season.

Don't forget your cap! **Baseball players always have something on their head.** If they're on defense, it's a cap or a catcher's helmet. If they're on offense, it's a batting helmet. In the dugout? They're mixing up their caps with everyone else's on the ground and under the bench. **Pro tips:**

- Use a sharpie to **write your kid's name on the underside of the bill on their cap and helmet** near the forehead edge. If the fabric or plastic is a dark color, use a silver sharpie.

- If you're on your way to a practice or a game, **learn to see an empty head as a naked head** and ask them where their cap is before you leave.

Undershirt

~ Optional, depending on age and jersey material
~ $10-$30

As players get older or play on more competitive teams, they may start to wear an athletic undershirt under their game jersey. If the uniform is more T-shirt style and/or athletic material, you may not need another layer. But, if your player is wearing more of a traditional jersey, a little looser and/or with buttons, an undershirt is a good idea. It's taken my kids time to get used to this idea, and my younger one still doesn't really love it. But it becomes more of an expectation as they get older. If they're worried about it being bunchy having two layers, get a more form-fitting, athletic/wicking material for the undershirt layer.

Cold gear - sleeves/thermal shirt

~ Optional if you live in... Florida or Puerto Rico?
~ $15-$60

This is less optional if you're in a climate where you'll be playing some - or a lot of - cold games. Your player should have a warm layer they can wear under their jersey. They won't be bundled up under blankets on the sidelines like you and I will. Ask the coach to see if they want all their players wearing the same color sleeves; they may prefer something neutral that doesn't stand out, like black. These can be actual separate "sleeves" - like 'arm socks' they can pull on - or it can be a thermal shirt to keep their core warm as well as their arms.

Cup w/underwear

~ Required once they're old enough
~ $15-$30

Boys usually start wearing a hard protective cup by around 10-11 years old, though some start earlier. This is particularly important for catchers; they may start wearing one a bit before the rest of their team due to the nature of their... position. When you're buying a cup, make sure to get the matching underwear with a pocket for the cup, to hold it in place. In our home, this item is known as "cup underwear". Regular underwear won't do the trick (one of our kids tried this in a pinch, and it didn't work well...). You can buy the underwear with the cup as a package or purchase them as separate items.

Once they start to wear a cup for games, have them wear it to practices too, to get used to it. Make sure they have it on before leaving the house. We've had to turn around more than once for a forgotten cup. Now when I ask if they're wearing it, they knock on it as evidence. Lol.

Sliding shorts

~ Optional
~ $10-$30

My kids have never wanted these, but some of their teammates wear them. It's basically extended length, beefed up underwear with a cup pocket - it could replace the above-mentioned "cup underwear". It has extra thickness/padding on the sides to provide some protection for their hips/upper legs when they slide.

Cleats

~ Eventually required

When my kids were young (5-8ish) and playing rec baseball, we multitasked their soccer cleats as baseball cleats. At younger ages, you could also get away with them wearing regular athletic shoes. Or, if you have hand-me-downs or are less stingy than I was, they can of course start wearing (molded or turf) baseball cleats at any age. However, once they get a bit older (9-10ish) and/or are playing on a more competitive team, cleats will be required. And possibly a coach-chosen, specific cleat in a specific color. This is coach/team dependent - some coaches don't care about color or brand, recommending whatever cleats are most comfortable for your player.

Molds ($40-$100)

- These are worn by younger players to provide extra traction when playing on dirt fields, though there is no real upper age limit. These have molded plastic "spikes" on the bottom rather than metal spikes. These may also be worn on turf, if you play on both turf and dirt and want to only buy one pair.

Metal ($50-$125)

- Most kids start replacing molded cleats with metal cleats when they're about 12, though this may vary a bit by league. They provide better traction than molded cleats on dirt, but can be dangerous for younger players.

- Be aware of rules about when/where they can be worn and **make sure your player has a backup pair of shoes** (molds, turfs, or even regular athletic shoes) in their bag. **They can't wear metal cleats on turf fields or some pitching mounds** because the metal spikes will tear them up.

Turfs ($50-$100)

- These look more like regular athletic shoes, as they don't have plastic or metal spikes, but they do have some extra texture on the bottom to provide more traction. They have better grip and are less slippery on turf than molds or regular athletic shoes but may not be required by your team until your player is older.

Stuff They Use

Bat

~ Required
~ $60-$500

The bat. The offensive weapon and status symbol that gets credited or blamed by your player for hitting performance. Bat envy is a thing, at least when players get to a certain age. Your kid may be full of hopes and dreams and "expertise" after binge watching YouTube videos made by self-styled bat testers, so they may want to influence bat choice. However, **there is some research to do and guidelines to be aware of**, as this was a more complicated purchase than I originally expected. There are different requirements depending on your player's age, height/weight, and league/division. **Prepare yourself for needing a new bat every year or two** as they grow and graduate into higher divisions with different requirements.

Certifications

- USA Baseball – The material and design of these bats limits the "pop" or trampoline effect compared to other bats. However, unlike BBCOR or wood bats, they are lighter weight and meant for use by younger players, aged 8-14. Since their performance is more muted, they're considered safer and are required by leagues including AABC, Babe Ruth, Cal Ripken, Dixie Youth, Little League, NABF, Pony League, and USA. My kids used USA Baseball bats when playing in rec leagues, as that is what was required.

- USSSA – These bats, also sized for 8- to 13- or 14-year-olds, provide additional hitting performance, meaning that they have more "pop" than USA Baseball bats. Some leagues or tournaments allow them; others do not. My kids (and all their teammates and opponents) started using USSSA bats when they joined competitive teams that play in tournaments, but **double check on your local rules before investing in what could be an illegal bat.**

- BBCOR – These bats are used by high school and college players, but may start to be required during 14U. Their performance is more similar to a wood bat, again limiting the "pop" or trampoline effect of the bat like USA Baseball bats do. But they're bigger and heavier, intended for older players who are bigger and stronger and hit further without the assist from the bat material and design.

- Wood – The OG. This is what pros use in the MLB. Most youth players won't use a wood bat during games. But they might use one during practice occasionally to increase strength, since wood bats are heavier than metal or composite. They won't dent, but they can break or crack.

Sizing

- Barrel width – This is another "be aware of the rules" measure. Certain leagues and ages have rules regarding maximum barrel width. Often this is covered by adhering to the above classifications required by your league, as each classification has limited widths, baking in some limitations. But it doesn't hurt to double check.

- Length – Measured in inches - 26" - 42"

  - **A couple of rules of thumb for finding the right length:**

    - If holding the bat vertically with their arm down at their side, your player should have one end of the bat reach their palm while the other end rests on the ground.

    - If holding the bat horizontally with the knob at their sternum and their arm extended to the side, the end of the bat should be in their palm and they should be able to curl their fingers over/across it.

- A lot of stores have charts that will tell you the best bat length based on your player's height and weight.

- Weight or 'Drop'

  - The weight of a bat is measured in ounces, but more important to know is a bat's 'drop'.

  - Drop = weight of the bat in ounces - length of the bat in inches

  - For example: a bat that's 20 ounces and 30 inches long would be -10, pronounced: drop 10. It's always

Age	Drop
4-6	-11, -12, or -13
7-8	-10, -11, or -12
9-10	-9, -10, or -11
11-12	-8, -9, or -10
13-14	-5 or -8
some 14U, High School & College	BBCOR -3

shown as a negative number. A higher drop (larger negative number, not closer to zero) is actually a lighter bat. Different age divisions will have different drop requirements. Players may be allowed to use a heavier bat ("playing up" to the next higher level), but not a lighter bat (which would be used by younger players).

  - What's the right drop for your player? **Check first to see if there are league or club requirements for your age group.** Then, within your allowed drop window, test a few bats to see what feels right to your player. **A rule of thumb here is for them to hold the bat straight out to their side. If they can hold it up for 30-40ish seconds, it's a good weight.** If that feels too heavy, have them try a lighter weight/higher drop (up to what is allowed by your league rules). If the required minimum weight feels too heavy, whelp, time for some push-ups.

Materials

- Composite (carbon fiber or graphite)

- Pros: Reduced vibration from hitting, large sweet spot and powerful pop

- Cons: Typically more expensive, needs to be broken in, not recommended in colder weather (below about 50-60 degrees) as it can become brittle and crack

- Metal alloy

  - Pros: Durable and balanced feel, good to go in any weather/temperature, is ready out of the wrapper: no break-in period

  - Cons: Smaller sweet spot and less pop, more vibration/sting

- Hybrid - a little of both of the above. Typically, a composite handle, to take advantage of its vibration-reducing qualities, and a metal alloy barrel, which brings durability and convenience, since it doesn't need to be broken in.

Get the insurance, register the bat with the manufacturer, and KEEP THAT RECEIPT. Take a photo of it, file it, stash it in your jewelry box, frame it and hang it on the living room wall. Set a calendar notice in your phone with its expiration date. When you get the miserable "my bat broke in practice" admission from your kid, it's a huge relief to realize that the dang bat is still covered by the warranty or insurance. Check your store and manufacturer's terms, but we've been fortunate to have bats covered three times. The timing of the bat breaking will determine whether it's still under the manufacturer's (usually 12-month) warranty, in which case you have to ship it to them for inspection and a replacement, or your store's insurance policy. If it's been more than 12 months but less than the expiration of the policy you buy, you'll file a claim through the store and you'll likely get a store credit. This credit may be for the original value of the bat you purchased or for a fixed dollar amount. In either case, it should cover at least most of the cost of a replacement.

Our bat casualties were caused by the following, all of which are apparently somewhat common:
~ Knob came off the end near the grip
~ Crack in the barrel
~ Dented

Don't take the plastic wrapper off the bat until you're 100% committed to it. Once that's been removed, most stores won't allow a return. So, if you're buying it as a gift, or just picking it up without your player, or you want to ask some additional questions before being locked into the purchase, resist the temptation to peel off that plastic.

Be aware that bats can have a limited lifetime. Using them in batting cages off machines can shorten their life if the machine is throwing balls denser than typical game balls or just because of the high number of hits. Consider having a back-up/practice bat to use on machines to extend the life of the game bat. If a bat loses pop or becomes damaged quickly, that could be an insurance claim, as described above, depending on the policy.

Gloves/Mitts

~ Required
~ $50-$400 each

Younger players can get away with an all-purpose glove until they're maybe 10-12ish, and/or start to play on a more competitive team. One exception to this may be getting a catcher's mitt if you have a catcher, though we've definitely seen younger teams with catchers using all-purpose gloves.

As they grow and play becomes more sophisticated, players benefit from more position-specific gloves. There are four main types:

- Catcher's mitt: This is thicker and has a deeper pocket to catch repeated pitches, perhaps at high velocity as pitchers get stronger.

- First base mitt: This is larger and wider than other infield gloves to scoop ground balls or catch the constant throws coming their way for routine outs at first.

- Infield glove: Smaller and shallower than other gloves, allowing for quicker transfer of the ball from the glove to their throwing hand to make a play.

- Outfield glove: Larger and deeper to allow easier catching of long fly balls.

Age	Catcher	1st Base	Infield	Outfield
7 & under	29.5"-30"	11.5"	8"-10.5"	9"-10.5"
8-10	30"-31"	11.5"-12"	10.5"-11.5"	10"-12"
11-12	30"-32.5"	11.5"-12"	11"-12"	11.75"-12.75"
13-14	32"-35"	12"-13"	11.25"-12"	12"-13"

As your player grows, they'll need larger mitts/gloves. When you're buying one, **get the largest size they can comfortably use** to get the most life out of it. Getting a new one requires not only treasure, but also time.

Your player got a new glove! Yay! It's super stiff and almost unusable! Yay! **Breaking in a glove is hugely important and a potentially long process.** It's hard to watch a player get to a ball and make an almost-great play, but the ball falls out of their glove because it's too stiff to squeeze it.

While it would be fun to watch a kid behind the dish trying to wield a three-foot shield of leather, no, catcher's mitts are not three times larger than every other mitt/glove. They're just measured differently. Other gloves and mitts are measured from the wrist edge to the tip of the index finger, measuring the material before it's all sewn together, so the finished measurement is a bit different. Catcher's mitts are measured by circumference.
shrugs

What's the right way to break in a glove? There's a lot of lore in this area, and all coaches/players/former players have favorite tactics. Should you get it steamed at the store to get started? There seems to be mixed reviews on this point. Steaming will soften it, but extreme heat can break down the material of the glove, which may shorten its life. This is a topic you can set your kid loose to research and layer their findings with common sense. You want to break in the glove, but you don't want to break it. Some ideas include:

- Sporting goods stores sell glove oil which can soften the leather, as well as mallets that can be used to beat the glove up a bit.

- Wetting the palm (not the fingers) with warm (not boiling) water to soften it. Then stretching, folding, and rolling the glove. Pounding the palm part with a mallet to start to form a pocket. Pounding the glove while it's folded together at different angles to loosen it up a bit.

- Wetting the palm (not fingers) with warm water, putting a baseball in the palm pocket, wrapping the glove around the ball, and holding it closed with rubber bands.

- Wrapping it up with a ball inside of it and leaving it in a hot car during the summer. Or sitting on it while driving in a hot car.

- Running it over with a car? I heard parents threatening to try this when we were at an out-of-town tournament and their kid's glove was new and still too stiff. It was good for a laugh, but whether it's a good idea is debatable...

- Playing a lot of catch.

Batting helmet

~ Required
~ $25-$80

Some leagues will issue this as part of the uniform, some do not. After seeing players get hit in the head by errant pitches and/or weirdly fouling it at themselves, its importance becomes evident.

Getting a jaw/face guard on the helmet is optional. This extra piece extends from the ear down the jawline on the side facing the pitcher while batting (so, this will be different for righties and lefties). It provides some extra protection, but if your player doesn't like it or feels too confined, it's not required.

Batting gloves

~ Optional
~ $20-$100

It's the player's preference whether or not they want batting gloves. Some may feel like they're a necessity. Others may not like them. They can help with grip on the bat, and can protect hands from blisters and calluses.

For what it's worth, my kids' old batting gloves end up worn out in the area between their index finger and thumb, where the bat has clearly rubbed through the glove material. Which is probably preferable to rubbing on their skin.

Sunglasses

~ Recommended / Required
~ $25-$225

While they indeed do need sunglasses to see the ball through bright sunlight and glare, they don't have to be Oakleys. They think they need Oakleys because "everyone else has them," but they don't.

Protecting their eyes from UV is of course important, and polarized lenses may be helpful. A wrap-around style can minimize sunlight coming in from the sides, and a flat top edge can help them fit under the baseball cap.

Catcher gear

~ Required for catchers
~ $150-$600

This protective gear is sold as a set and includes a helmet, chest protection, and leg guards that cover the knees and shins. If you're on a more competitive team, ask your coach if they want the gear to be a certain color to match your uniforms. You're usually safe getting black gear, which is neutral and nondescript. The gear comes in sizes indicated for a several-year age range and is somewhat adjustable, so it could last for a few years if bought when your player is on the younger end of the stated range for that size. The helmet size may determine which size set to buy - they'll have corresponding hat sizes in the product description. Try to avoid getting gear that is too big. Chest protectors should fit like a shirt - if they're hanging too loosely and flopping around they can be a distraction for the catcher.

Wrist guards - for catchers

~ Recommended for catchers
~ $15-$40

These are short stretchy sleeves that have a hard shell on one side. For some brands at least, when you first get these, you'll activate the shield part of the guards and have your kid wear them around the house for a specified amount of time - it will mold to the shape of your kid's wrists and harden. After this initial set up, a player pulls them on past their hands to cover and protect their wrist area when blocking balls. This will save a lot of bruising on their wrists and the lower part of their arms.

Knee wedges/savers/blocks - for catchers

~Optional for catchers
~ $30-$50

These are foam wedges or blocks that strap to the back of catcher's calves, giving them something to kind of sit on while squatting. They somewhat decrease the angle of their squat and may reduce stress on the knees. While I'm sure my creaky knees would appreciate these, my catcher kid thinks other catchers who wear them are cheaters. :) To each their own on this one.

J-Bands

~ Required when kids get a little older (11ish) and start throwing with greater velocity.
~ $35-$40

These bands are used to strengthen and condition the rotator cuff and surrounding muscles. Players use them for exercises at the start of each practice and before each game for arm health.

Flat glove

~ Coach-dependent
~ $30-$60

These are used for practice drills. Rather than catching a ball, the ball bounces off it. Some coaches may want players to have these, others won't.

Elbow guard

~ Optional
~ $30-$110

This item protects a batter's elbow from errant pitches. This isn't required but could be helpful to protect from injuries, particularly for kids who are less likely to tolerate being hit by a pitch and/or when pitching velocities increase as kids get stronger.

Sliding glove

~ Optional
~ $50-$60

a.k.a. The Oven Mitt. This protective item can be worn by players who want to look ridiculous while running the bases. :) While they're starting to become more common, I've never bought one and fewer than half of our teammates use one. It will allegedly protect one's hand and fingers while sliding and could be helpful in some situations, especially to protect a hand with an existing injury. Its most frequent contribution to the game is the ump calling time while a runner and their first base coach fiddle around with getting it out of the runner's back pocket, taking off batting gloves, and putting it on. I'd call this item truly optional: if you or your kid are more comfortable with them wearing one, they are available.

Bag - shoulder/backpack or catcher/roller

~ Required
~ $25-$120 for a backpack style, $50-$275 for a wheeled catcher's bag

There's a lot of stuff on this list. Your player needs somewhere to put it all so they can carry it around. Most players who aren't catchers will have a backpack-style bag with vertical bat pockets on the sides. Due to their extra protective gear, catchers use wheeled duffel bag-style bags.

Note: Players (not moms) should indeed be carrying their own gear around. It's a point of pride and responsibility. *They need a little help when they're young to load it up without cracking a car window with the bat, but for the most part, gear schlepping is on them.*

Ask around to see if your league or club requires that you buy a bag through them before buying one on your own. Buying through them will almost always be more expensive, sometimes by a lot, but some leagues/clubs may require a team logo embroidered or printed on the bag. I think for our teams we were technically "supposed" to buy through them... but we had catcher bags that were plain black, the organizations' bags weren't logoed, and nobody ever questioned it. However, some may be stricter than others.

Make sure the bag is big enough for everything they need, particularly catchers. When our bag was too small, we stood around for 1,000 years after every game waiting for our kid to Tetris all his gear back in there. However, if you're going to travel at all with the bag, you might want to consider your favorite airline's rules for maximum standard checked luggage size when picking one out to avoid oversize bag fees, if possible.

Stuff For Practice at Home

Tee

~ $20-$130

There's not really a lot of differentiating technology here. You just need one that will hold steady at different heights without falling down; sometimes if they're too loose they'll "telescope down" when you don't want them to. There are some with a more flexible ball holder at the top, so that if it gets hit by the bat there's less interference.

Net

~ $60-$150

Theoretically, the benefit of a net - usually about 5'x7', give or take a couple feet - is to limit where balls can go when practicing hitting off a tee or throwing (i.e. saving the neighbor's siding/windows/windshield). It also makes collecting the balls a lot faster. Some nets have a built-in strike zone target to help when practicing pitching. Pro tip: set up the tee pretty close to the net (just a few feet back) to catch all but the craziest of fouls.

Rebounder

~ $30-$150

This is a vertical or angled trampoline-ish net for a player to practice throwing for accuracy (there's usually a built-in target) and catching it when it bounces back. This solves the problem of: "Turn off the video game, go outside, and practice." – "But mom, there's no one to throw with."

L-screen

~ $100-$400

Want to pitch or soft-toss to your kid so they can practice hitting? Awesome! Want to avoid a line-drive to your face once they really learn how to hit? You want an L-screen to hide behind. While there have been some entertaining (for me) moments watching my husband hit the decks to dodge a ball our kid nuked right back at him, it is definitely safer to use one of these.

Bucket of balls

~ Individual balls are about $3-$9 each.
~ You can get a bucket of 24-30 for about $75-$150, depending on the type and quantity.
~ (I know. Barf. For balls?!?)

While these are mainly for at-home practice, have your player keep a couple in their bag for warm-ups before practice and games, if needed.

Baseballs are all the same, right? White leather, red laces, fits in the palm of your hand? By looking at them, one would think so. But, no! There are all different kinds, made with different materials to specs for different ages and leagues.

The take-away here is that it is important to check what you're picking up, because baseballs are all about the same size and look pretty dang similar, but they aren't. If you have a little one, you don't want them practicing with high school balls, because if they get hit with one, it's going to hurt a lot more. Once they're a little older, it probably doesn't matter that much what they're hitting off the tee. Just know that there is a difference.

- Safety baseballs - for 3-6 year olds in tee ball - they are softer and lighter

- RIF (reduced injury factor) and SEV (severity) Index ratings

  ○ Level 1 - a bit firmer than safety balls, designed for 5-7 year olds, but often used by 6 year olds, after tee ball

  ○ Level 5 - a bit firmer still, designed for 8-12 year olds, but often used by 7 year olds

  ○ Level 10 - firmer yet, designed for ages 12 and up

- Youth tournament baseballs are a little less dense than high school or college baseballs, but they're not soft.

- High school and college baseballs are a little lighter than MLB balls, as they're designed to be hit with metal bats, not wood.

- Synthetic/fake leather baseballs (vs. actual leather) are cheaper than game balls and a bit lower quality, but work fine for practice. They actually do better in wet weather because the synthetic cover doesn't absorb water the same way real leather does. One note on these balls - they aren't recommended for pitching machines, as the synthetic material isn't great for the machinery.

- The "Official League Baseball" stamp means that the

ball meets the specs (size, weight, etc.) for whichever league/level is indicated.

99baseballs.com has an incredibly extensive list of ball recommendations by age and league, as well as a bunch of info on how a ball is made and what's inside. I bet you never thought about this before, but now you're curious, aren't you?

Once you have baseballs, they tend to hide and then show up in weird spots, with car cup holders being among their favorite domains.

Pro tip: Check for baseballs in the grass before mowing the lawn. Just do.

Chapter 4
Scheduling

F or some reason, baseball seasons have always felt busier than other sports seasons, on both rec and club teams. But how much of your life it will truly monopolize depends upon what level you're playing. We'll take a peek at what this looks like on the annual scale for 30,000-foot view planning, as well as what a weekly schedule could look like during the season.

Annual Scheduling

Let's start with the big picture. Baseball season is traditionally in the spring and summer. There may be some exceptions, with communities playing at other times due to local conditions. For example, some hot-climate-people may play through the winter to avoid melting at the field during the summer. And/or to stay in baseball shape year round, thereby smoking those of us who live in a climate with four seasons during March tournaments. However, most leagues/teams/clubs hold their primary season between about March and July/August.

Rec Teams

The season for rec leagues often runs 8-10ish weeks, covering a shorter segment of time within that spring/summer window. Some start practice as early as March, others not until May. The flexibility of playing just in the summer can be nice if your player is busy with another sport or activity in the spring. Check to see what's available in your area and what works best for your family.

Registration for rec leagues is typically several months before the season starts. If you're thinking about playing baseball, start looking into it earlier than you think you need to (by November for March-start or January for April/May-start) so you don't miss a deadline. Some leagues also offer an early bird registration discount! While you might be able to register late if there are still spots available, some leagues do fill up early.

Competitive Teams

On a competitive/tournament team? Just go ahead and clear your calendar. You have weekend plans starting about March 1 for the next four to five months. Competitive practices will start sometime in the fall or winter, typically at least a couple of months before the first games.

Tryouts for competitive teams are early. Really early. Some are before the prior season is even over. Yes, for some teams, the tryouts for a season that starts practicing in January for games that start in March could be **the prior June or July**. Remember 'silly season' from Chapter 1? This is it. Tryouts, offers to stay, cuts, and jockeying for spots all starts shortly before a season ends and extends perhaps a few weeks after. Not every league/club holds their tryouts so early, but many do. There are often opportunities to join teams late (we did!), as they have players fall off their rosters for a variety of reasons. But, you may have to dig deeper to find those spots.

If your player is going to join a competitive team, it's important to **be willing to commit the time and prioritize showing up for practices and games**. Certainly, life happens. Perhaps you had a family trip on the books before you joined a team. Or there could be an important event like a wedding you can't miss, or, God forbid, some kind of emergency. But, when it's in your control to make informed scheduling choices, try to plan vacations or other big events before or after the season. Some coaches will ask the team early on about any known conflicts to try to plan tournaments around them from the get-go. Whether you have that opportunity to weigh in or not, **if you do have something on the calendar that will cause your player to miss a game, let the coach know right away**, even months in advance, if possible. If multiple families will be out the same weekend and the coach isn't able to plan accordingly, **the rest of the team may have to forfeit if they don't have enough players.** Regarding practice, missing every once in a while will happen during a long season. But your kid's not going to get better if they regularly skip practice. They may miss important guidance, fall behind in their development and conditioning, and may feel less connected with the other players. It's not good for them or the team that's counting on them.

Fall Ball

What about 'fall ball'? As mentioned in Chapter 1, it's basically off-season baseball and is typically more casual. While teams always strive to win, the fall season is often seen as an opportunity to practice and develop for the main season in spring/summer. A lot of baseball players take the fall off to play a different sport and let their throwing arms recover, but some like to continue playing during that time.

One note for fall ball: when trying out or registering, you'll do so according to your player's age **the following spring/summer season**, not according to their age for the season they just completed. You can look at it as starting the next season early, not extending the current year's season. Registration/tryouts for fall ball varies a lot. Some clubs/leagues will automatically offer a fall ball spot to anyone selected during summer tryouts for the following year's spring/summer teams. Some have separate tryouts earlier. Some just have open registration up until a couple of weeks before practice starts, usually in mid-August.

There will of course be some variation, but here's a general rule-of-thumb guide.

Year at a Glance

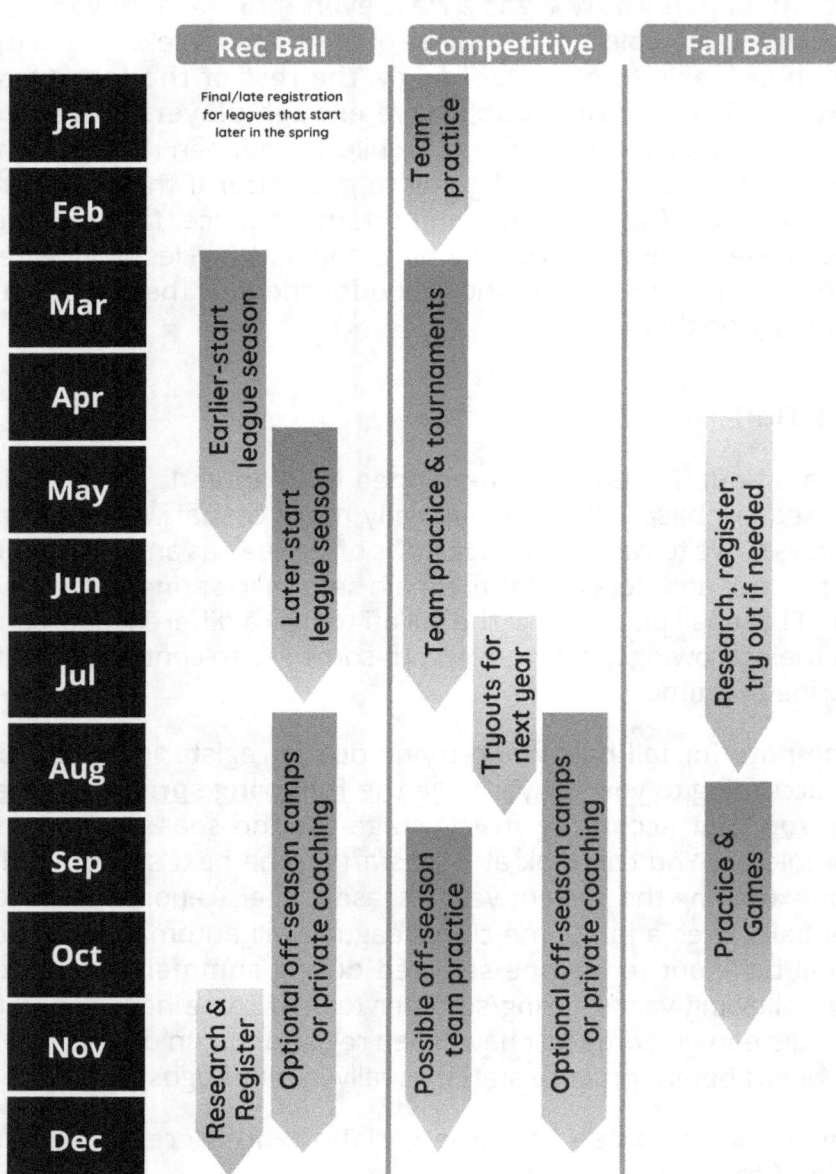

	Rec Ball	Competitive	Fall Ball
Jan	Final/late registration for leagues that start later in the spring	Team practice	
Feb			
Mar	Earlier-start league season	Team practice & tournaments	
Apr			
May	Later-start league season		Research, register, try out if needed
Jun			
Jul			
Aug	Optional off-season camps or private coaching	Tryouts for next year	
Sep			Practice & Games
Oct		Possible off-season team practice	
Nov	Research & Register	Optional off-season camps or private coaching	
Dec			

Weekly Scheduling

Rec Teams

Rec teams will likely start their season with **two or three weeks of practice before games start**. During those initial weeks, the team may practice two or three times per week, working on basic skills and an understanding of the game. Once games begin, teams usually practice less. There are often one to two games and one or two practices per week. Unless the league runs a mid- or end-of-season tournament, or if they're trying to squeeze in a make-up game that was canceled due to weather, **you'll likely play one game on game days**, whether a weeknight or weekend.

Competitive Teams

Competitive teams **typically start formal practices at least two months before the first tournament**, and practice two to four times per week. Some teams may also do strength and conditioning training in addition to team practices, depending on club policy or coach preference.

Once tournaments begin, weeknight practices will likely continue, but weekends become the domain of tournaments. **Let's talk about tournaments.** Weekend tournaments will have pool play on Saturday and bracket play on Sunday. What that usually means is that **you'll have two games scheduled on Saturday - the times and locations of which you'll find out a week or two in advance**. The team's success (or not) on Saturday will inform their seed for Sunday's bracket.

Expect to not know the time for your first Sunday game until sometime on Saturday night when the last of the pool play games are done and the bracket is released. Your coach may distribute the bracket or your first game info to the team, and/or you may be able to find and follow the bracket on the tournament's website or app. Having Saturday dinner with teammates? The kids (and parents? lol) will probably be following the last games of the night trying to predict how they'll seed depending on how those last games go.

Sunday is usually single elimination. If your team plays at 8:00 a.m. and loses, they're done. You now have the rest of the day free to do laundry, take a nap, or... do anything other than baseball. Unless the coach is miffed about how the team lost (were they sloppy or lazy?) and schedules an extra practice for that afternoon. On the other hand, if they keep winning (go team!), you'll keep playing until they either lose a game or win it all. **Depending on the size of the bracket, you could play up to three or four games on Sunday if your team is doing well.** See Chapter 5 for your "moving to the field because we live there now" checklist.

Don't expect games on Saturday or Sunday to be back-to-back. While sometimes they will be scheduled one right after the

Example Bracket

Play well on Saturday? Your Sunday journey could start here. You'd start later in the day and only need to win two games to win the championship.

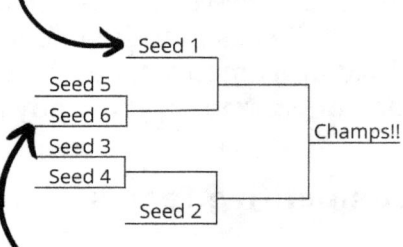

Play not-so-well on Saturday? Your Sunday journey could start here. You'd need to win three games and get past the 1st Seed to get to the championship game. This is a lot harder. The team will be more tired, and you may be in trouble with pitching, depending on how many pitchers your team has available.

other, there will often be breaks between, which has pros and cons. A break can offer an opportunity to rest and refuel, and to have a mental reset if the first game didn't go well. However, if the team is on a roll, a break may slow the momentum. For better or worse, be prepared for the possibility of breaks extending your time at the field.

Some tournaments - typically the ones you travel to - are longer and more of an event. There could be exhibition games (that don't factor into the tournament bracket), more days of pool play games, extra skills events, and/or double-elimination brackets.

See some "off weekends" in your schedule? Check with your coach on what that means before you plan a camping trip. Sometimes those weekends are on hold for make-up tournaments, in case prior tournaments get canceled due to weather.

Delays

Game start times are kind of estimations. The first games of the day will start on time, weather dependent. However, as you go later in the day, the likelihood of games starting on time decreases. Remember how "game times" are minimums, and teams need to finish innings once they start? Delays caused by late or long games accumulate; the start times of the following games on that field will domino forward, with late afternoon games sometimes starting an hour or more later than scheduled. Some leagues and tournaments do a better job of mitigating this than others by building in scheduled breaks between games to help absorb overruns. If there's heavy rain, lightning, or other hazards, play can be delayed for hours, pushing everything back. Schedule changes don't always happen. Sometimes game times will behave, with all variables staying in their lanes and marching along nicely. But there are days when the schedule goes off the rails altogether. **It's helpful to have an open mind and an open calendar to reduce stress**.

Scheduling Tools

Your team or league probably has an app they use for scheduling. It could be TeamSnap, GameChanger (which is also used for scorekeeping), SportsEngine, or something similar. You want this app. If a spouse initially registered your kid for the league and they're the one automatically linked to your player on the app, ask them or the coach to add you, too. If you're on there first, add anyone else in your household who needs updates. **The app** is often used by coaches or team admins to share important information via the calendar, email, and chat features. **Turn on all the bell and whistle notifications and check it regularly** for anything you may have missed: you're going to want to be aware of canceled practices, changed game times, or other updates as soon as possible.

Many of these apps will have a feature that also allows you to sync the events in the app (practices, games, team pictures, etc.) directly to the calendar on your phone. Do it. This might be my favorite technology assist of the decade. We're all busy, and it's hugely helpful to have all the team events automatically populate - and update - themselves in my calendar. How does this work? Each app is a little different, and as they release updates they might change a little. But look for the option to sync to your calendar: it could be clicking an icon with an up arrow or found by going into settings. Then subscribe to the schedule/calendar. Sometimes it may not immediately show up in your phone's calendar, but it should once all the network/server gremlins get their ducks in a row, within an hour or so max.

Have a neighbor or friend on the team who lives nearby? Meet a new family on your team who lives close to you? Meet your new best friends!! **You should schedule a carpool with them. Immediately.** Baseball can be a lot, whether you're on a rec team or a competitive team, and taking one or more days of kid taxi service off your calendar in exchange for helping shuttle around others is a huge help. You could keep it simple and have a certain day of the week when you always drive. Or, if your team's calendar (or your family's!) has a lot of moving pieces that causes who drives when to be a little less standardized, **a shared online spreadsheet can keep track of who is driving which day**.

Chapter 5
Game Day

It's game time.

All the registrations, and research, and tryouts, and buying stuff, and driving, and practices, and team meetings, and, and, and.. is all for this. Game day.

It's time to pack up and roll out. Woo hoo!

Arrival Time

Typically coaches want players to **arrive at least 30 minutes early to warm up**. As players move to older or more competitive teams, **the coach may want them there an hour or more before game time**. Arrival time may be included in the calendar on your team scheduling app, so look for that. If it is - great! If it's not, during a practice or in a team chat, check with your coach at least a day before the first game to see what time they want the team to arrive.

While some coaches are more relaxed about pre-game arrival, and may stroll up a few minutes late themselves, others may bench a player for an inning or more if they don't arrive *at least* 10-15 minutes *before* the stated arrival time. If you're new to a team, try to get a feel for this expectation from the other parents and plan accordingly. If everyone's new, **consider getting there 10-15 minutes before the stated arrival time for the first game**. Is the coach already there getting set up and waiting for the team? Gold star for being on time! Now you know to adjust actual arrival time to earlier than what's posted. Twiddling your thumbs at the field by yourself for 10-15 minutes before anyone else gets there? Well, at least you weren't late, and now you know for next time.

After the kid has been delivered to the field, you may have some time to kill, especially if there's more than an hour until the game starts. Prior to early-morning games, you may run into half the other parents on your team at the nearby coffee shop. It can be fun to chat and spend time together! I've found this window is also a good time to run by the grocery store if there's any food or other items you need for the day.

Stuff For Your Player

- Everything identified in Chapter 3, plus...

- A *large* water bottle - with their name on it, if they're not too old and cool for that

- Food, especially if you're playing more than one game. Whether it's a meal or snacks, consider food that's higher in protein and lower in sugar until after they're done playing. Sugar crashes mid-game are a drag.

- Sports drink with electrolytes for hydration, particularly on hot days. Like the food, see if you can find lower-sugar options for use before/during games.

- Crocs, slides, or other comfortable shoes, if they want to change out of their cleats before, after, or between games

- Sunscreen - applied before they join the team for warm-ups, but send them with a bottle/tube to reapply if they'll be playing for many hours

- Weather-related gear to wear during warmups or between games, if needed: hoodie, rain jacket, coat, etc. For hot days: cooling towels in ice water.

Stuff For Families

How much you really need to haul to the field depends on how many games you're playing, and where. Playing tee-ball or a rec league, and have one game on a weeknight or Saturday afternoon? Just bring a chair, a beverage, sunscreen, and any weather-related needs. Maybe some snacks, because why not. Playing tournament ball, with three to seven games per weekend? You're going to need and want more than that. Also important: Is the field you'll be playing at nice, with shaded seating, a snack bar, and real actual restrooms? Or does it just have aluminum bleachers from 1962 and one poorly maintained port-a-potty? You may not know until you get there, so be prepared for the latter.

Wagon

- After a couple years of sherpa-ing armfuls of chairs and other gear between the car and the field, I finally caved in to wagon use. Ours is a foldable red one that was originally used for pulling small children around the neighborhood or the zoo. Now it has a new life as a stuff hauler. There are some pretty sweet double decker ones with space for chairs to slide under the main cargo area for anyone really committed to wagon efficiency.

- There is often an impromptu wagon parking zone behind the bleachers or a little behind where spectators set up chairs next to the field. They're ideally nearby, so that all the families can access what they've hauled in while keeping them out of the prime seating area around the backstop.

Chairs

- Bleachers are comfortable for about three minutes, and tolerable for maybe one game. If you'll be at the ballfield a lot, invest in something more comfortable. You won't regret it. Cup holders and pockets are handy accessories.

Picnic / Sports / Camping Blanket

- If your field is at a park with grassy areas surrounding the diamond, you could spread out a blanket on the ground for seating. This is easier to pack in than chairs and can be a nice alternative if you have a little one who needs a place to sit with toys and snacks.

- This seating option is less enjoyable at fields surrounded by asphalt and dust.

- It can be repurposed as an extra layer against the elements on cold, wet, and/or windy days.

Got Siblings?

- With any luck, there will be other siblings on the team, and together they will form a playground gang to entertain themselves during *endless* (in kid time) baseball games.

- For days when the gang isn't there, or when they get tired of each other, it can be helpful to have something for them to do. Bring a favorite toy or three, crafts, a book, a ball and glove if they're an aspiring player themselves, and as a fall back a trusty old screen of some sort because mindless entertainment is better than fielding constant questions about if the game is over yet.

- And of course snacks. All the snacks.

Cooler

- Use a wheeled one, especially if it won't fit in your wagon with the other stuff.

- If it has wheels and some straps/pockets, the cooler may be able to replace the wagon if you're just heading out for one game. Drinks, snacks, and miscellanea inside. First aid equipment in front pocket. Jackets and an umbrella strapped on top with the built-in bungee cords. Chair slung over your shoulder. Or maybe just use the wagon.

Stay-Warm Stuff

- Attending early-season games where it's *actually* snowing? Or feels like it could? Or it's clear and sunny, but you can see your breath and the water fountains haven't been turned on for the season because it's still *freezing*? I see you.

- Standard issue: coat, hat, gloves, fuzzy socks, coffee, blanket. Sometimes long underwear as a base layer.

- Upgrade options: There are some amazing wearable sleeping bags that I'm always envious of. There are heated chairs. There are straight up heaters. Some people get sports pods - those individual clear plastic tents. While I see the advantage of the shelter, it feels a little separated from the action, family, and friends for me. To each their own.

- Layers in general. Even for warm days when it's chilly in the mornings and evenings but blazing hot mid-day.

Stay-Dry Stuff

- Because the game will go on if the field is playable and the weather is not severe

- Umbrella

- Rain jacket

- Pop-up canopy - also see below

Stay-Not-Cooked Stuff

- Sunscreen

- Brimmed hat / baseball cap

- Sunglasses

Pop-Up Canopy

- It's an oasis from the sun, rain, or foul balls, and a gathering place for families during or between games.

- A collection of families' canopies makes a fun pop-up-city! The team may pile in with the families while killing time between games.

Water

- Some fields have nice water bottle filling stations. Others have nothing. Be prepared if you've never been to a specific field before and you have more than one game there. Pack in what you, your player, and the rest of your player's cheering section will need, especially on hot days.

- Consider using a multi-gallon water cooler for refilling water bottles.

Food

- Meals: If you're going to be at the field for the day and want to avoid eating out all the time, and/or if your game(s) are stacked up over mealtimes and you don't want to miss any action, consider packing in easy/portable meals. **See Chapter 9 for a few ideas.**

- Snacks

Phone

- You'll have it anyway, but it may be heavily used for photos, videos, and keeping an eye on the score

Portable Charger

- Running GameChanger on your phone - whether as scorekeeper or as a spectator who can't remember the count or the score (me) - is a battery killer. Especially if you have three or four games in a day.

Hand Sanitizer and/or Wipes

- For those port-a-potty situations

First aid

- Consider having a few things on hand for common injuries, like from sliding or being hit by pitch. You may not need this stuff every game, but it can be helpful to have it on hand:

    ~ Band-Aids - variety of sizes, but particularly larger ones
    ~ Gauze & medical tape
    ~ Wound cleaning solution &/or wipes
    ~ Ointment
    ~ Actual ice or instant cold packs
    ~ Advil/Tylenol
    ~ Hydrocortisone
    ~ bug bite/sting relief

Planning Ahead

This may just be me, but trying to get everyone and everything we need out of the house on time on game day is enough brain damage without trying to figure it all out at the last minute. Planning ahead became more important when we joined a competitive team and were basically packing out for the whole damn weekend. But preparation was helpful in rec, too, especially if we were running out to a weeknight game right after getting home from school and work, or threading the needle to get there amidst other weekend activities.

- **Establish departure time**. Where are you going and how long does it take to get there? Likely traffic? Need to stop on the way for anything (food, coffee, gas...)? Factor in time for people running back inside for forgotten stuff of the jacket and water bottle variety, and disappearing to go to the restroom when you're trying to load the car.

    ○ **Departure Time Math** = Arrival time - minutes

expected to arrive before arrival time - travel time including traffic - stops on the way - slowpoke factor

- **If it's not perishable, load it up early**. Way early. Like the day before. Or, if there's room, just leave stuff in the car when you can: your player's baseball gear bag, chairs, wagon, pop up canopy, etc. When you do need to unload it, have a dedicated space/pile for game day stuff so you don't have to hunt it down every time you reload it. Way early.

- Make sure cooler **ice packs are in the freezer the day before you need them**. Because they like to hide forgotten in the bottom of the cooler all week until you need them again and it's time go and they're warm, dammit.

- Similarly, make sure your **portable charger is juiced up**.

- **Meal planning**. Considering game times, what meal(s) should you pack in, or plan to pick up on the way, between, or after games? Snacks? **A few packable meal ideas are included in Chapter 9.**

  ○ Have a weeknight game? If you don't want to eat out, **consider making a to-go dinner in advance,** so you can just grab it out of the fridge after school/work and roll. Slow cooker meals can be a stress-saver, too. Toss the ingredients into the pot in the morning, let it cook all day, and it will be ready to scoop up into to-go containers to bring to the game. Or, if your game is late afternoon or early evening, it can be waiting for you when you get home.

  ○ Have an early morning game across town? **Consider prepping a to-go breakfast the day prior.** Something that's easy and quick to reheat, or that you can just grab and go.

  ○ Going to be there for lunch? It feels like this is always

a sandwich. Could be something different. Probably should be sometimes. If you need to be out of the house before sunrise, **consider making the sandwiches the night before** to avoid adding that task to the morning sprint. Or, have your kid make them while you enjoy your morning coffee.

- **Dedicated snack bag/cooler.** Non-perishable snacks and drinks/water bottles can just hang out in a bag and be refilled as needed throughout the season. Throw perishable stuff with ice packs into the waiting cooler when it's time to go.

- **Ice**. Slow ice maker in your abode? Consider emptying your ice reservoir into a plastic bag a day or more ahead of time. Keep your bagged ice in the freezer while your ice maker gets to work on refilling the reservoir. Or buy bagged ice to keep on hand. We seem to go through a lot of ice on hot game days, between water bottles and the water cooler. If the weather is warm, you could also consider filling and freezing a second water bottle for your player (and family members!); they can drink the second one as it thaws out. Frozen water bottles can also serve as extra ice packs in the cooler, if needed. Just leave a little space in any water bottles you freeze so the water has room to expand and it doesn't blow up.

- Does your team do **post-game snacks? Is it your turn?**

Where to Sit Etiquette

It is generally accepted etiquette that parents and fans will sit on the same side of the field as their team's dugout. I know I don't want to listen to people cheering in my ear when my kid strikes out. While they're (usually) just supporting their kids as we do ours, I'd much prefer that parents on the other team do that "over there" on the other side of the field. And I'm sure they'd prefer that I do my cheering over here.

But what if it's nicer over there due the shade tree or whatever? No - we're not invited there. Our team will luck out with shade some other game.

What if we set up camp before we knew which side our team would be on? We need to move.

What if we have friends on the opposing team and want to sit with them? Of course, we should! Baseball can be a small world, and running into friends and hanging out with them at the field is a great time! But, out of respect for everyone sitting around us while we're over there, we need to keep our own cheering on mute. We should also try to keep our wagons, etc., out of the way and defer prime seating to the parents of that team.

Whoever is scoring the game/running GameChanger gets first choice for seating - both so they can see plays and hear the umpire, and as a thanks and deference for them taking on the responsibility. It's a big job. More on GameChanger below.

What about the neutral DMZ behind the backstop? Imagine a line coming from the umpire straight out of the field and keep to the half closer to your team's dugout. And, everyone sitting there should be on their best behavior as positive team ambassadors due to close proximity to the opposing team's families.

Is the prior game still going on the field where our team plays next? We need to wait out of the way. If there are big bleachers and lots of extra room, we can sit and hang out - sometimes it's fun to watch other games while waiting. We've spent time with some nice people from other teams who we've supported or who joined our cheering section until their kid's game started. But it's best not to really crowd in with our chairs and tents and coolers and wagons until the prior game is over and their families are moving out.

~~Mom Zone~~

Stay. out. of. the. dugout. Once you drop your player off for warmups, they should be on their own with the team and the coach(es) until after the post-game team chat. Meaning, don't enter or linger around the dugout, and don't talk to your kid through the fence, as it can be a distraction. The coaches will want their attention focused on warmups, watching the game, preparing for a play, and/or supporting their teammates. Unless your player or a coach approaches you to ask for something (water refill, first-aid item, etc.), or there is some kind of major injury (a doctor-required injury, not a Band-Aid or ice pack injury), hold your position as sideline spectator unless Coach waves you over. Make sure your player has sunscreen applied, plenty of water/sports drink/snacks (if needed/allowed), and weather-appropriate clothing/gear **before they go to join the team for warm-ups**.

If the coach is herding a team of little ones, they may ask for help during warm-ups or to manage dugout chaos during the game. There is more flexibility on this point in the younger years, but err on the side of staying out of the team space and follow the lead of the coach.

You Want GameChanger

I've mentioned this term offhand a few times already, but what is GameChanger? It's a wizard of an app that serves several functions. There's a free version that provides all of the most important features. You can also pay to upgrade for some other cool tricks; you'll decide whether they're worth it or not. Your team GameChanger king/queen can add you as a family member if you aren't on there automatically, so that you can see all the team's and your player's info. Once you're in, you can then add additional family members, as well. There will be a new team profile in the app for each season, so your scorekeeper will need to add you each year. Even if you're on the same team with the same coach for several years, seasons are separated in the app. It's fun to look back on prior seasons as your kid progresses!

GameChanger's primary use by most teams is for scorekeeping. Each team will have a parent who, God help them, will be tracking every play throughout the game. They program in the batting lineup and position of each player each inning. They note every ball, strike, homerun, error, double play and which positions assisted... everything. If you know baseball and have laser-focused attention, your team could use you for this. It can be helpful to have more than one person who can run GameChanger, both to cover for each other if somebody has to miss a game, and just to give them time off if they want it.

My younger kid's team had a failure of redundancies in GameChanger coverage and somehow I ended up as the scorekeeper for two games. Luckily, my older kid was sitting next to me and we tag teamed it; between the two of us we were able to keep track of what was happening and figure out how to plug in unusual plays. The experience increased my already-big respect for the heroes who do this for us every game, and a new appreciation of the snarky-but-real shirts that say, "Do Not Disturb. I'm running GameChanger."

The app does other helpful things, too. Like TeamSnap and other apps, it can be used for scheduling practices, games, and other team events, as well as messaging. But perhaps my favorite feature is that it lets you follow a game live even if you aren't present. There will inevitably be conflicts with work schedules, sibling schedules, or other life stuff that keeps you from making it to a game sometimes. You can track the game as it's happening on GameChanger in a few ways. The primary way is watching the GameStream, which shows an animated graphic of a field that notes who is where and the outcome of each play as it happens. And let's be real - I have GameStream on when I'm sitting right there at the game, too. I use it as a scoreboard. It helps me keep track of the score, count, where we are in the lineup, what inning we're in, etc. While most fields have a scoreboard standing around in the outfield, very few actually use them.

If your GameChanger person has the equipment and is willing, they can also broadcast live video of the game through the app. This feature has been a favorite of our team grandparents or other family members who live out of town or can't make it to every game but want to watch. The video broadcast is often done by attaching a phone to the backstop, which serves as the video camera. One can also buy a specialized camera designed to sync with GameChanger, because of course you can. **Beware: if you're seated near the GameChanger broadcast camera, it also captures sound**. So, your conversation with the mom sitting next to you about... anything... will be shared with whoever is watching the live video feed or recording. I may or may not have received texts from my mom during games letting me know she could hear me...

You can also check out the competition on GameChanger. You can't see specifics about their players other than first names (which is good - privacy of minors and all), but you can see their team record and schedule. It can be fun to watch your own team nerd out as they check the record of their upcoming opponents, make predictions of bracket seedlings by watching other teams/games in their tournament, and more. They're little sports analysts in the making.

All the stuff above is included in the free version of the app as of this writing, and it's awesome. There are additional fun tools in the upgrade/paid version. Some find it useful to shell out for it. Others don't. Some of the upgrade features include:

- There's a feature called GameStream Radio that will narrate/call the game - it's basically an AI voice that verbalizes the plays as they're plugged in by the scorekeeper. I love listening to this if I'm driving around elsewhere and can't look at my phone to see what's happening.

- Since everything is noted in the app as it happens and every action is assigned to each individual involved, the app keeps statistics. While **these are only as accurate as the scorekeeper and, as mentioned earlier, aren't all that meaningful for young players**, they can still be fun to explore. Some basic statistics are included in the free version, but it's more extensive in the paid version.

- GameChanger can also be connected to a Pocket Radar, which is a device that measures the speed of pitches. So, if you have a pitcher and someone has connected a Pocket Radar to the game, the app will note the speed of each individual pitch throughout the game. Pitch speed stats aren't all that important until a player gets into high school, but can be a novelty starting around 12U.

- If there's a livestream video of the game, it is also being recorded. You can access the entire game recording if you missed it or want to rewatch it. The app will also tag video clips of specific plays; it doesn't get every single one, but it gets most. The clips are tagged both to the plays in the game rundown and to the individual players involved. So, you can go to your player's name in the team roster, go to the video tab, and see all their clips. It's easy to record or take pictures of your kid's at bats on your own if you want to, because they're predictable. But it's harder to get defensive plays on camera because they happen quickly and unexpectedly. You're able to download video clips from GameChanger, which is awesome when there's a particularly great play you want to keep.

Photos and Videos

Whether you're taking photos or video clips to send to grandma, to brag about your kid on social, or to build a highlight reel for college recruiting, you'll probably want to capture the experience now and then. It can be helpful to know your kid's comfort with and reaction to being photographed while playing. It makes some kids nervous to see someone taking pictures; in that case, it can be helpful to be more incognito so we don't get in their head when they're trying to play.

Some kids don't care or notice whether you're taking pictures or not. My oldest wants to know where the hell I am if I'm not right up on the fence every at bat with the lens positioned for an unobstructed view. It's a distraction for him if I'm *not* taking video, because he likes to study his own film to see how he did or how he can improve, and of course so he can watch his highlights over and over. ESPN hasn't called for them yet, but you never know.

Pro tip - **when you're recording, try to bite your lip to keep from yelling and cheering** when you'd normally yell and cheer. You'll have to listen to yourself cheering every time the clip is replayed. Ug.

Sometimes when a fellow mom is away, I'll try to get video of her kid's at bats, and other plays if possible, to send to her. I know I hate to miss games, and love to get little glimpses of how my kid did if I'm not there. I usually record other kids from my seat, being sneaky with my phone, as I don't want to make that teammate uncomfortable.

At the end of the day, try to review any photos and videos you've taken and delete all but the keepers. This is easiest to do if you "heart" or "favorite" a great play right after you record it. Otherwise, you may end up with a hundred million video clips of at bats taking up gigabytes of space on your phone and in your cloud account at the end of the season. You can either select all and delete (gasp) or spend a year and a half re-watching and deleting most of them anyway (death by videos).

Rain Delays

These are a bummer and annoying but they're part of the experience. Weather may interrupt a game or delay the start of it for a few minutes or a few hours. If the delay is due to lightning, expect to be sent to your vehicle for safety. **Games can resume on short notice. So, if you leave the field don't go far and keep an eye out for communication from the coach when you've got the all-clear** (by text, app message, or knocking on car windows). Sometimes, if the weather is extra bad, games are suspended and will resume another day. Or, especially in tournaments which are time-bound to a weekend, they could just be cancelled altogether.

Rub Some Dirt on It

Sometimes kids get hurt playing. Most of the time it's relatively minor and can be fixed by an ice pack, a bandage, or some rest. Whether getting scraped up while sliding, getting a nice bruise from a hit-by-pitch, running into the fence while trying to catch a pop fly foul, or something else, little injuries happen almost every game. Hence the first aid kit in the packing list.

Generally speaking, baseball is (usually) a low- to no-contact sport. With the exception of trying to tag out a runner - which is sometimes enthusiastic and dramatic - players themselves are usually some distance from each other.

According to the American Academy of Pediatrics[1] , with the exception of swimming, cross country, and track & field, baseball had the lowest incidence of concussions in boys' high school sports. By a lot. All other sports had 2x (basketball) to 18x (football...) as many as baseball. The trend was similar for softball among girls' sports.

According to another report[2] , when comparing all injuries requiring a doctor's visit and at least one day away from play, football is again the most injurious high school sport with 3.96 injuries per 1,000 "athletic exposures," with an "athletic exposure" meaning one player attending one practice or game. Baseball was the least at 0.89 per 1,000.

1.
https://publications.aap.org/pediatrics/article/144/5/e20192180/38225/Concussion-Incidence-and-Trends-in-20-High-School?autologincheck=redirected

2.
https://www.medpagetoday.com/meetingcoverage/aaos/103500#:~:text=%E2%80%94%20And%2C%20no%20surprise%2C%20national,football%20is%20the%20most%20injurious&text=LAS%20VEGAS%20%2D%2D%20Annual%20surveys,the%20lowest%2C%20researchers%20reported%20here .

While baseball/softball had fewer overall injuries than other sports[3], some of them can be quite serious. Whether due to encountering a hard ball moving at a fast speed, an unfortunate twist, or a collision, baseball isn't without risks.

According to Children's Health[4], **some of the most common baseball injuries are actually due to overuse**, especially for pitchers. Those injuries include Little League Shoulder, Little League Elbow, rotator cuff issues, and injuries to the Ulnar Collateral Ligament, which is repaired with the infamous "Tommy John Surgery." **Risks from overuse is a major reason why playing other sports in the offseason and taking time off from throwing is recommended for youth athletes.**

A 10-year follow-up study[5] of 481 youth pitchers aged 9 to 14 found that, "Pitching more than 100 innings in a year carried 3.5 times higher odds of serious arm injury compared with those who pitched less. Other risk factors for injury: higher velocity pitching, bigger (taller, heavier) athletes, pitching while fatigued, and specializing in baseball young rather than playing a diversity of sports."

While hopefully it is minor and will improve with rest and some stretching or conditioning exercises, if your player is complaining of pain or discomfort in their elbow area or shoulder, it may be worth having it peeked at by a doctor. It's not worth risking long-term health to play through what could be a more serious injury. In most cases, you'll get the all-clear, peace of mind, some guidance on how to care for a throwing arm, and maybe what specifically to look for in the future that would indicate a more serious problem.

3.
   https://www.hopkinsmedicine.org/health/conditions-and-diseases/sports-injuries/sports-injury-statistics

4.
   https://www.childrens.com/health-wellness/common-baseball-injuries-and-how-to-prevent-them

5. https://pubmed.ncbi.nlm.nih.gov/21098816/

In the event of any injury that will prevent your kid from playing for any length of time, find a time to chat with the coach as soon as possible after your medical appointment. This will allow you to be on the same page about when the player will be available again and what the doctor-specified recovery plan looks like, including possible restrictions along the way. This will help ensure your player is phasing back into the game in the right way, and it allows the coach to plan accordingly and secure a guest player if needed while your kid is out.

Any significant injury can be heartbreaking for our players – and for us! – as we watch them navigate pain, physical recovery, and frustration with not being able to play. We lament not having a magic wand to heal them up and get them right back to doing what they love. To minimize an injured player's feeling of loss, it can help for them to stay connected with the team. They can still go to practice and help out the coaches. They can still go to games and be the 'bat boy', head cheerleader of the dugout, and/or perhaps even acting first base coach if an actual coach thinks they're up for the promotion. Staying integrated with the team by being present can ease their transition back into the lineup – likely to the jubilant cheers of their teammates who they've continued to spend time with along the way.

Moms Against Assholes

"Little League baseball is a very good thing because it keeps the parents off the streets." - Yogi Berra

Alright friends, let's get on the same page here. Maybe it's always been this way and I've just dialed in as I've spent more time at the field. But what the actual hell is going on at youth sports games? While, thankfully, many games are normal and at least mostly civil (a little bit of chirping is part of the game), some are infused with a seething rage. Real and crazy rage from some people. Parents sniping at opposing parents. At the ump. At the opposing coach or their own coach. And, worst of all, at the kids on their team and the other team. Some coaches are getting fired from leagues due to bad behavior. Police are sometimes called because of fist fights – or worse – between opposing parents or coaches. It's. **Youth**. Sports. While it really is glorious to see a deserving jerk get ejected and sent packing to the parking lot by an umpire (Yeah Blue!), it's at best eye-rolling, and at worst scary, to watch adults behave this way. The other team is not the enemy. If we ran into them under other circumstances, we'd probably bond over our shared experience of youth baseball and wish their players the best of luck. It's a game. **For kids**. It's supposed to be fun.

Why do we sign up our kids to play baseball? Because they love it? So they can get exercise? Make new friends? Try something new? Learn to be coachable and work collaboratively with a team? Because they have MLB dreams (hey, you never know!)? All of the above, or something else? I'd venture a guess that it wasn't because we can't wait to spend our weekends stressed out and angry, spitting fire at everyone around us. We've all seen this. Maybe it's been us sometimes. Let's do better. Let's be an example for other parents and be the role models we want our kids to emulate. Helping them learn how to be good sportsmen, how to lose with grace, how to win with humility, and how to persevere through adversity with honor. Because they're watching us. All of us.

We're going to disagree with coaches sometimes. We may believe our kid deserves more playing time, or should be at a different position, or that the coach should be doing any variety of things differently. Unless a kid's safety or wellbeing is in imminent danger, give it 24 hours. Most in-game complaints become forgettable non-issues after sleeping on it. However, if there is a larger issue or pattern that you feel is important to discuss with the coach, schedule a time to chat on an off day. It's so much easier to have a productive conversation, to preserve a positive relationship with the coach, and to actually resolve an issue, or at least come to a mutual understanding, with cooler heads. There could be context or background we aren't aware of. Or... maybe an issue or conflict really is a huge deal and unresolvable; maybe the coach is the asshole who we don't want as a role model for our kid. If that's the case, it will be easy to walk away and find a new team during the offseason.

We're going to disagree with umpires sometimes. Being horrified by calls is as American as apple pie. Umps are going to call that outside-by-a-mile ball a strike, and they're going to call your kid out at home when his slide clearly beat the tag by at least a full second. An initial moment of collective exclamation at a particularly bad call – "What?!?!" – may be a reflex reaction. We may quietly grumble in commiseration with fellow parents, but we have to keep the volume low and get over it. Yes, we all want to see justice in the world, especially for our kids. But parents arguing with an ump is always a losing proposition. They're definitely not going to change their call, and they'll probably just start feeling salty toward a team that's yelling at them, poisoning the water for future close calls. There's a shortage of officiants in youth sports because they're tired of our shit, so they quit, and I don't blame them.

If there is a major issue with a rule violation, or perhaps the field ump had a better view on a play than the home plate ump who made the bad call, let the coach handle it. They may have established a positive rapport with the ump at the start of the game and can (hopefully) talk it through in a productive and professional way that has a chance of actually reversing the call. Sometimes umps will indeed overturn their call after a discussion. Most times they won't. But, in the grand scheme, the outcome of any given call - or even the game - really doesn't matter. Our reaction to it, though, does.

I remember a game we were losing. It was not pretty. We were making mistakes and the opposing team was very talented. Despite all of this, our boys were happy, smiling, and having fun. Why? Because the kids on the other team were super nice, as were their parents and coaches. The boys on our team and theirs were friendly to each other on the field, complementing each other, joking, chit-chatting. It was glorious, and I wish it was something we experienced every weekend.

The Post-Game

The game is over. It was a spectacular win or it was a disappointing loss. It was an exciting close one or it was a blow out. The team's post-game debrief with the coach just wrapped up and your kid approaches. You've just spent the last couple of hours - at least - watching their game(s) unfold, and you can't wait to talk to them about.... If they're hungry and want to stop for something. What music or podcast they want to listen to on the way home. If they want to play a board game tonight or watch a movie.

What??

According to a survey by some long-time former coaches[6], **most college athletes' worst memories from youth sports were the post-game car rides**. Being immediately peppered with questions about the game, well-meaning advice, criticism of something they should have done differently, comments about coaches, teammates, and the ump - they don't want to hear any of that from their parents, especially not in those moments right after the game ends. Kids often need some distance from the game immediately afterward to process. **They want your relationship to transition from athlete-spectator back to kid-parent**.

So, what does that look like?

They walk up. "Hey bud! You hungry?" Maybe a side hug and kiss on the head. You can walk or ride quietly for a bit, or chat about whatever else you may have chatted about if a game hadn't just happened. **If and when _they_ bring up the game and want to talk about it, then we can follow their lead**. We likely will indeed spend time talking baseball and debriefing with them. The

---

6.
   https://www.thepostgame.com/blog/more-family-fun/201202/what-makes-night mare-sports-parent

important point is to let them bring it up when they're ready. And, of course, as we've transitioned from spectator back to parent (Right? It's so hard.), we'll likely approach the conversation differently.

If they're angry or frustrated, we may start by just listening while they get it off their chest. After they've blown off some steam and cooled down a bit, and if they want to talk about it, we can engage in conversation and standard parenting (i.e. – no, the ump isn't the Antichrist, everyone makes mistakes, things we can control vs. things we can't, etc.). Or, if they just needed to vent and don't want to talk baseball, we can talk about what's for dinner.

If they're wallowing in self-criticism for a play they missed or striking out, we can encourage and support and ask if they'd like us to practice with them before the next game. If they're super hard on themselves, we may need to talk through forgiveness and grace not just for others, but also for themselves. And to remember and celebrate the things they did well or improved on since last time, because the good stuff can get overshadowed if they're focused on their mistakes.

Or, they may be riding high if they had a great game! Then we'll obviously congratulate them and their team on a job well done and find a way to celebrate! Just not so much that they get a big head or get complacent about practice. :)

At the end of the day, what do they want and need to hear from us the most? Love and support. Just like always. **Before the game, they don't need coaching from us. They need, "Good luck, have fun, I love you!"** The time for coaching and advice has passed. Come game time, they need the mental freedom to execute on what they know and practiced without last-minute - likely unintentional – pressure from us. **During the game... this is a question to ask of them.** Do they like to hear us cheering, or is it distracting? What kind of cheering? Would they rather we be quiet? **Unless we're the actual coach of the team, in-game guidance is a no-no.** The only exception to this I've heard from my catcher-kid is if he's frantically looking around and can't find the ball and I'm right there and see it, he wants me to tell him where it is (usually: "Up, up!" if it popped straight up. Or "Feet, feet!" if it got underneath him.). But, other than generalized words of encouragement for him and his teammates, that's it.

The thing they want to hear from us the most? **"I love watching you play."** Because obviously we do. And they want to hear that more than anything else.

Chapter 6
Traveling

Traveling together with a team is the best! There's a sparkliness and excitement that surrounds the experience of playing games on the road. For the players, it's like going on vacation with their friends to play a game they love. Travel glows on the game calendar like a promise of adventure and glory, and the anticipation grows until it's time to pack the bags. Now-grown former youth athletes often say travel ball was one of the highlights of their childhood.

Coaches may choose to book out-of-town tournaments for a few reasons (other than it being awesome). For teams in states with cold winters, traveling somewhere warm in February or March provides early season games that aren't at risk of being snowed out. Traveling also broadens the field of available competition, allowing your team to try their hand against teams from other parts of the country. Sometimes you may actually end up playing against teams from your hometown - this has happened to our team a few times - but just being away from home makes even that more exciting. And, of course, traveling is fun! The kids love it and it can foster closer friendships between players through the experience. This may translate to better teamwork on the field... and just having more great friends in their lives!

Booking It

As soon as your season schedule is finalized and your team is officially registered for an out-of-town tournament, travel planning will likely begin. Someone will help with coordination -

usually one of the moms. This could be you if you enjoy planning travel!

Lodging

It's usually easiest - and the most fun! - if the team stays together at the same hotel. Being in the same spot can also help with pre-game coordination. The coach may have all the players meet in the lobby or the parking lot by a certain time and have a few parents shuttle them over to the field for warmups. This also gives the rest of the families a little more time to make their way to the field closer to game time. Or each family could certainly just get their own player to the field by warm-up time like they would for a local tournament. **If there will be a morning carpool for the team, it's best to organize it in advance** so drivers are prepared and the drivers' family members can hitch a ride from the hotel to the field with other game-time-arrivers.

While most trips are planned in advance by your coach, some travel could pop up at the last minute. Depending on the league you're a part of, if you play in a state championship tournament and end up in the top two or three finishers... Surprise! You're going to Dodge City, Kansas, in two weeks for regionals! Do well there? Surprise! You're going to Florida for nationals! Super exciting for the team! And hope you didn't have other plans!

Some tournaments are "stay-to-play", meaning that the tournament organizers have partnered with a specific set of hotels where visiting teams are required to stay. These lodging options are listed on the tournament website, and your team will "unlock" access to book rooms through their site once you're registered to play. Often rooms in these hotels offer discounts, and there can be plenty of acceptable options. If there is not an acceptable hotel option, your team can opt out of the stay-to-play requirement. But there is a fee to do so, usually a few hundred dollars. Your team will need to decide if it's worth the fee to stay elsewhere. If it's not a stay-to-play tournament, your team can stay wherever you'd like!

Your team travel planner can organize a block of rooms - in a stay-to-play hotel or elsewhere - to temporarily save space for everyone. If the hotel isn't already offering discounts through the tournament for individual bookings, a room block might. You'll just need to make sure you book your room before the block expires and the rooms are released to anyone else trying to book.

Depending on the tournament's rules and location, another lodging option is renting condos in the same complex, or collectively renting one or more large houses for team families to stay together. It can be cost-effective, delicious, and fun to have family-style or potluck dinners for all the players, parents, siblings, and coaches. It's easier to do this with access to kitchens and somewhere to comfortably hang out. Team party!

Flying?

Depending on the nature of the trip and timing, **families may fly on their own or everyone may try to get on the same flight**, at least on the way there. When we've traveled for spring trips, families typically travel on their own, as they're managing if/when to pull kids out of school a bit early to catch a flight. Your team/coach can try to schedule trips to overlap with spring break, but if there are kids on the team from different school districts with different calendars, this can be impossible. When we traveled to Cooperstown during the summer (which is its own amazing animal of an experience!), the team traveled together on the same flight there, but families made their own way back home.

If you have an ambitious and organized team travel planner, they can book all the tickets at once, increasing the likelihood of the kids getting to sit together. Or families can book the same flight on their own. Either way, with a large group traveling together, the plane starts to feel like a semi-private charter. It can be fun for the players to wear matching team jerseys or practice shirts, showing connection with and pride for the team while traveling together. If the kids are the polite and respectful people we know they're capable of being, maybe the pilot will even wish the team luck during an announcement over the intercom!

Whether you're driving or flying, you'll want to make sure you **arrive by the night before the first day of games, at the latest**. While you may not end up playing until later in the day, like local tournaments, you probably won't know game times until a week or two prior, and could end up with that 8 am game on the first day. **Some tournaments require the team to be there for check-in by a certain time the day prior** - find out in advance what the requirements are and plan accordingly.

Regarding the flight home, check the tournament website for when the final championship games could end on the last day. If possible, you could consider staying that last night after the tournament and leaving the following day. If your team is doing well, **having a late flight or extra night of hotel booked removes the we-need-to-get-to-the-airport-is-this-game-over-yet stress**. If you end up being done earlier in the day, you have some extra time to explore wherever you're visiting. If the tournament ends on a Sunday and you're trying to get home in time for work and/or school on Monday, try to book the latest flight you can. While you may not expect your team to play in the championship, you never know! We've had teammates' parents calling airlines to change to later flights in the middle of games because we were playing longer than expected and they didn't want to miss the last game!

Road Trip!

Windshield time is a special way to bond and make memories together. The forced togetherness often leads to sharing an inspirational view, experiencing a new culture or landmark, or even just chatting and having a good laugh about something crazy that happens. Because something crazy always happens while traveling. Whether it's the Grand Canyon or the World's Largest Ball of Yarn, if you're traveling more than a few hours there's likely one or many stops of interest to explore between home and your tournament. Traveling as a dynamic duo with just you and your player, with other family members along for the ride, or even caravanning with other families on the team would each create unique experiences and stories.

Road Trip Checklist

- Do a little research in advance to see what's fun or interesting on the route between here and there. There's always something. Map it out and plan your departure time accordingly to allow for stops along the way there or back.

- Download an audio book, podcast, or music to listen to, especially if you'll be passing through a remote area with limited radio options.

- If you don't already have some favorite car games, look up a few in advance, or some fun/funny/thought provoking conversation prompts.

- Snacks. Obviously.

- Maybe have non-drivers pack a pillow for when they inevitably fall asleep.

Budget Checklist

In Chapter 7 we'll dive a little deeper into this and lay out some more comprehensive budgeting tools. But the main costs to consider when planning travel include:

- Lodging = # rooms x # nights

- Airfare if flying x # family members attending

- Possible checked bag fees if flying (you'll need at least one, as the bat can't be carried on)

- Rental car if flying

- Gas if driving

- Daily allowance for food and drinks - consider bringing some from home if driving

- Activities - What's in the area that you don't want to miss? Possible team events, like group tickets to a game?

- Incidentals - parking, tolls, souvenirs, etc.

Depending on the timing of the trip, your budget, and your family calendar, you'll decide whether any other family members will attend or whether one parent will travel with the player. Team trips can be a fun family event, depending on your situation and who is available! But, especially if you're not driving to your destination, having more people attend is also a larger expense. If your player has siblings, you'll need to weigh possible conflicting events, who can miss school and/or work so they can go, and other considerations. But, if the tournament is during summer break or butts up against the start or end of spring break and you have some free time in your schedule, you can make an adventure of it!

Group Activities

While the players, families, and coaches spend a lot of time together at practices and games, going out of town brings that to a new level. Traveling creates so many opportunities to hang out with the baseball family, whether it's having breakfast together at the hotel buffet, team dinners, or hanging out at the pool after games are over for the day. It really brings the team together, both the players and the families.

Team dinners may not be every night while traveling, but usually happen at least once. If going to a restaurant, a mom usually does some research to find a place with seating for a large group and makes reservations in advance. If you can find a casual place with a bunch of outdoor seating and yard games, you win. Or everyone can chip in and order a bunch of pizzas to have at a nearby park or the hotel. Or, if you're staying at a place with kitchens, the families can organize meal sign ups with everyone chipping in coordinated food items. Pizza parties and potlucks can feel more leisurely than going to a restaurant. Going out together is still great but can feel more time and space limited depending on the establishment. Driving in and staying at a place with kitchens? Maybe bring crock pots to allow food to cook all day while you're at games, and it'll be ready to go when everyone gets back. This works great for taco meat, chili, etc.

The team may also want to do stuff together beyond eating and playing baseball. Depending on when and where you're traveling, you could see if there are MLB spring training games or minor league games where you could get a large block of tickets. Some youth tournaments are hosted in locations with other baseball events, like the College World Series in Omaha, Nebraska, each June, which could also be fun to attend as a team. There could also be a water park, an amusement park, a beach, or another fun attraction nearby! You'll just need to **wait until your game schedule has been released before buying tickets** to anything, and you'll want to **build in a time buffer** because game delays will game delay. Event planners will also want to **coordinate with the coach, as they may have plans for team practices** you'll want to work around.

Logistics & Packing

So, all that stuff in Chapter 3? How does all that get where it needs to be, especially if traveling by air? It's definitely easier to travel for baseball by car - just throw it all in the back like normal and add some suitcases - but it's possible to get the essentials to your destination when flying, too.

While some items will need to be checked when flying, especially the bat (I know - say a prayer for the wisdom and mercy of baggage handlers), try to carry on what you can. **Definitely carry on anything your player must have that's difficult or impossible to replace on short notice, <u>especially uniforms and</u>**

gloves/mitts, as well as anything else that's TSA compliant and fits.

There are (of course) bags you can buy that are designed to safely transport bats. Or you can wrap it up in towels or clothes and nestle it among other items packed in a large suitcase or catcher's bag.

An abbreviated checklist of game day stuff for tournaments on the road:

- Your player will need all their regular game day gear, but pre-travel is a good time to evaluate what's riding around in their gear bag. Are there a bunch of extra balls, duplicate/old items, or empty snack wrappers from two months ago? Help them clean out and downsize to the essentials before hitting the road, especially if flying.

- Thin/packable shoulder bag for water bottles, sunscreen, snacks, and other items you'll want at the games

- Pack a water bottle for each traveler: full and somewhere handy in the car if road tripping, or empty and in carry-ons if flying. You can fill them on the other side of security to avoid paying airport prices for something to drink. And you'll have them for the games.

- Sunglasses, hat, and sunscreen, plus cooling towels for your player if you'll be somewhere hot

- Travel umbrella and rain jacket

- A warm layer, if the mornings or evenings will be cool, or if the weather looks suspicious

- Sports blanket, if you have room

- Portable charger - make sure to juice it up before leaving home

- Hand sanitizer/wipes (because port-a-potties are

everywhere)

- Maybe a handful of Band-Aids and one or two instant cold packs

- if uniforms will be worn more than one day, pack a Fels-Naptha bar (see Chapter 9 for info on this magical object) and a laundry detergent pod in a Ziploc. Or, the kids can just play dirty while on the road...

After your kid lays out & prepares to pack their uniform and other wearable baseball gear, **do a double and triple check with them for items from head to toe: CAPS, jerseys, undershirts (if needed), hoodie (if needed), pants, belt, cup underwear, sliding shorts (if they use those), socks, and CLEATS.** For some reason caps and cleats are easier to forget than the rest. Or maybe that's just us. We've almost forgotten them several times and actually did get to buy a shiny new pair of cleats in Phoenix once on our way from the hotel to field. Yay. If your player promises they're in their gear bag, double check.

Special Trips

A few tournaments operate on a different level, like a weeklong baseball camp with a tournament as the centerpiece. The most well-known of these is in Cooperstown in upstate New York, which is exclusively for 12-year-olds. Others, in Branson, Missouri, and elsewhere, host multiple ages. For these events, the team stays in dorm/bunk room accommodations on-site, like a sleep-away camp but with coaches as counselors, bless their hearts. Food (of varying quality) is often served cafeteria-style. And there may be other fun activities, events, and skills competitions, in addition to the tournament games. Families stay off site but drive in to be spectators for games and other events. While parents may bust the players out for a team dinner or two with the families, it's fun for them to stay on-site most of the time to soak up the experience.

Some events have a tradition of team pin trading. **Each team will have a unique pin produced ahead of time (job for a mom...) and each player will get a set amount**. The team will plan for this at the start of the season and build the cost in with the team fees. They'll probably want to keep one of their own team's pins and use the rest to trade with kids they meet from across the country, coming home with a fun collection. **They may need a small towel (that you are done with forever) or a pin book with fabric pages to store all their new treasures.**

What your player will need may vary by location, but a basic packing list could include:

- Sheets and a blanket or sleeping bag

- Pillow

- Uniform - all items (jerseys*, pants, socks, belts, caps*, cleats, cup)

    ○ *Some of these tournaments will issue their own jersey shirts and caps to be worn at games, so you may not need those items

    ○ Some tournaments may also require pants to be a specific color or length, and/or have color requirements for belts and socks. For Cooperstown, we needed white knickers, a blue belt and socks, and a red belt and socks to accompany the jersey shirts they issued.

- All game gear - bat, gloves, protective gear, etc.

- Regular clothes (shirts, pants/shorts, socks, underwear), shoes, and pajamas

- Toiletries and tote: shampoo, soap, toothpaste, toothbrush, deodorant (please...)

- Towel and wash cloth

- Shower shoes / slides

- Glasses/contacts if needed

- Laundry bag

- Charger for phone (if they have/need one), possibly with an extension cord and/or surge protector (to create extra outlets for teammates in case wall outlets are limited)

- Name on EVERYTHING. Like even underwear and socks. Every. Thing. **Pro Tip: Use a silver or gold sharpie for dark colored fabric**

- Snacks and water for the kids to have in their bunk room, if allowed

- Funny care package for coaches: Febreze or air freshener, ear plugs, some kind of "I survived" T-shirt

- Team pins for trading, and something with which to collect those they receive

The Next Level

If your player is on a team that travels a LOT, and/or when they get to be older, meaning closer to or in high school, the team will likely travel on their own with their coaches. Without the parents and siblings. Soak it up while you can. There may be ways to follow the team remotely, perhaps with games being broadcast through a tournament app or website. Shed a tear for the end of an era.

Chapter 7
Finances

The cost of youth baseball can be stupid. For better or worse, it's become a whole industry. While there are some great opportunities for player development with more sophisticated clubs catering to ever younger players, the ratcheting-up of related expenses for many competitive-level teams can make it cost prohibitive for many families.

But, when our kids really love something, we'll do all we can to find a way to make it work. Because we're moms. And moms are badass. Let's roll up our sleeves and get to work.

We've looked at different elements of this already in different chapters, but let's pull it all together now and figure out how to deal with it. How much money you'll invest depends on the kind of baseball experience you're looking for, your player's age, and whether or not you're traveling. Playing in a rec league is a lighter financial lift. Competitive is a much heavier investment, but nothing is impossible. Some expenses are required, others are more negotiable or optional. Each family should be clear on all financial expectations and obligations up front to make sure they're comfortable and have a plan before committing to a team. Baseball isn't fun anymore if the cost is stressing the family out.

Budget Planning Worksheet

Included below is a budgeting tool, which includes ballpark (I mean, this pun had to be used somewhere...) estimates for each category, as well as a few columns for you to pencil in actuals as you research teams in your community and shop around for gear.

Details on all of the stuff listed below – like whether you really need it and what to look for when shopping – is included in Chapter 3.

Keep in mind that some items can be used for multiple seasons, until they break or your kid grows out of them. **The cost estimates on the sheet below account for having to buy all new gear**. So, the cost for equipment at least may be a little to a lot lower once you have some things on hand.

First, a few definitions of the annual costs for participation.

Registration

Level-dependent
~ Rec/League – $25-$500
~ Club - $1,500-$3,500+

Registration is the basic "joining the team" amount for a season, and covers practices, the coach, and, for rec & league teams, games. If you're joining a club, registration does NOT include games, but may cover some other benefits like use of the facility. Since clubs are a much larger expense than a rec or league team, they often offer the option of paying in monthly installments to make the cost easier to digest.

Team/Tournament Fees

~ $800-$3,000+
* This estimated cost range is for competitive/club/travel teams. But **a rec or league team could have some modest team fees as well if you're registering for a tournament or two, or if you're purchasing anything as a team.**

In addition to the cost of registering with the club, your team will have fees to cover the cost of tournaments and, if your coach isn't a parent of a player, coach travel: typically hotel, per diem for food, and airfare, if applicable. This budget will also capture any other extras that you may pay for collectively, such as a team banner, first aid items to keep in the dugout, additional matching shirts for practice or travel, pins for trading, etc. **These fees are required as these costs are above and beyond team/club registration, and can be substantial, sometimes matching or even exceeding the cost of registration. Make sure to ask about estimated team/tournament fees when shopping around for teams.** This amount can vary wildly depending on the variables listed above, especially the number of tournaments and coach travel. These fees will be accounted and paid for by a coach or a volunteer parent. You should be notified of the finalized amount of team fees by around the time practice starts, once the coach firms up the tournament schedule.

Example Team Fee Budget:

- 10 tournaments at $700 each = $7,000

- Coach travel = perhaps two trips at $1,200 each:
  ~ 4 days per trip at $50 per day for food = $200 per trip
  ~ 3 hotel nights per trip at $200 a night = $600 per trip
  ~ Flight = $400 per trip

- Team banner = $200

Adding it up: $7,000 (tournaments) + $1,200 (coach travel 1) + $1,200 (coach travel 2) + $200 (banner) = $9,600 total for the team
If there are 12 players on the team: $9,600 / 12 = $800 per player

---

Again, all the numbers above are just an example to illustrate what team fees could cover and how a player's portion is calculated. Actual team fees will vary a lot from team to team, and season to season. If your team registers for special event tournaments, like Cooperstown which includes room & board for the team, those are a lot more expensive and will significantly increase team fees.

Annual/Seasonal Expenses		
Expense	**Estimate**	**Actual**
Registration	**Rec/League:** $25-$500 **Independent:** varies - between Rec & Club costs **Club:** $1,500-$3,500+	**Option 1** **Option 2** **Option 3**
Team Fees *Typically not needed on rec teams, but verify. Includes tournaments, coach travel, and other shared team expenses.*	$800-$3,000+	**Option 1** **Option 2** **Option 3**
Total		

Uniform		
Expense	**Estimate**	**Actual**
Rec/League Player - A La Carte Items *Jersey & cap often provided by league*		
Pants	$10-$60	
Belt	$5-$20	
Socks	$5-$20	
Competitive/Club Player		
Uniform Package	$200-$500+	
All Players - Cleats *Just Molds - OR - Molds + Turfs - OR - Metal + Turfs*		
Molds	$40-$100	
Metal (when allowed)	$50-$125	
Turfs (if needed)	$50-$100	
All Players - Additional Stuff to Wear		
Cup w/underwear	$15-$30	
Undershirt	$10-$30	
Cold weather shirt	$15-$60	
Sliding shorts	$10-$30	
Total		

Game Gear		
Expense	**Estimate**	**Actual**
Bat	$60-$400	
Fielding glove ** all players, incl. catcher*	$50-$400	
Batting helmet ** if not included w/uniform*	$25-$80	
Batting gloves	$20-$100	
Sunglasses	$25-$225	
Elbow guard	$30-$110	
Sliding glove	$50-$60	
J-bands	$35-$40	
Flat glove	$30-$60	
Backpack	$25-$120	
Catchers - Additional Items		
Catcher's mitt	$50-$400	
Catcher's gear set: helmet, chest protector, leg guards	$150-$600	
Wrist guards	$15-$40	
Knee wedges/blocks	$30-$50	
Wheeled bag	$50-$275	
Total		

Practice Gear		
Expense	**Estimate**	**Actual**
Tee	$20-$130	
Net	$60-$150	
Rebounder	$30-$150	
L-screen	$100-$400	
Balls *one individual to a higher-end bucketful*	$3-$150	
Total		

Player Development		
Expense	**Estimate**	**Actual**
Camp *could be every day for a week or a few hours a week for several weeks*	$150-$350 per camp	<u>**Option 1**</u> <u>**Option 2**</u> <u>**Option 3**</u>
1:1 Coaching	$50-$100 per hour	<u>**Option 1**</u> <u>**Option 2**</u> <u>**Option 3**</u>
Training for strength, speed, or agility	varies; perhaps $100-$200/month	<u>**Option 1**</u> <u>**Option 2**</u> <u>**Option 3**</u>
Total		

Travel - Trip 1		
Expense	**Calculate**	**Actual**
Airfare	(Roundtrip flight cost) x (# people)	
Checked bag fee	(per bag fee) x (# bags)	
Rental car	(daily rate) x (# days)	
Hotel	(nightly rate) x (# nights)	
Gas	((roundtrip mileage) / (average mpg)) x $ per gallon	
Food & Drinks	(daily budget) x (# people) x (# days)	
Activities	(cost per activity/ticket) x (# people)	
Airport parking	(daily rate) x (# days)	
Uber/Lyft/Taxi	To/from airport? Use at destination?	
Parking at destination (hotel, activities, etc.)	Estimate - Cost per night? Per activity?	
Other: tolls, souvenirs, etc.	Guesstimate as needed	
Total		

Travel - Trip 2		
Expense	**Calculate**	**Actual**
Airfare	(Roundtrip flight cost) x (# people)	
Checked bag fee	(per bag fee) x (# bags)	
Rental car	(daily rate) x (# days)	
Hotel	(nightly rate) x (# nights)	
Gas	((roundtrip mileage) / (average mpg)) x $ per gallon	
Food & Drinks	(daily budget) x (# people) x (# days)	
Activities	(cost per activity/ticket) x (# people)	
Airport parking	(daily rate) x (# days)	
Uber/Lyft/Taxi	To/from airport? Use at destination?	
Parking at destination (hotel, activities, etc.)	Estimate - Cost per night? Per activity?	
Other: tolls, souvenirs, etc.	Guesstimate as needed	
Total		

Travel - Trip 3		
Expense	**Calculate**	**Actual**
Airfare	(Roundtrip flight cost) x (# people)	
Checked bag fee	(per bag fee) x (# bags)	
Rental car	(daily rate) x (# days)	
Hotel	(nightly rate) x (# nights)	
Gas	((roundtrip mileage) / (average mpg)) x $ per gallon	
Food & Drinks	(daily budget) x (# people) x (# days)	
Activities	(cost per activity/ticket) x (# people)	
Airport parking	(daily rate) x (# days)	
Uber/Lyft/Taxi	To/from airport? Use at destination?	
Parking at destination (hotel, activities, etc.)	Estimate - Cost per night? Per activity?	
Other: tolls, souvenirs, etc.	Guesstimate as needed	
Total		

Adding it all up!		
Expense	**Estimate**	**Section Subtotal**
Registration	Rec/League: $25-$500 Independent: $500+ Club: $1,500-$3,500+	
Team Fees	$0-$3,000+	
Uniform items & other stuff to wear	$100-$850	
Game Gear *for new items, if needed*	$180-$3,000	
Practice Gear *for new items, if needed*	$250-$1,000	
Development *optional, a la carte*	varies	
Travel	varies	
MINUS (woo hoo!) expected fundraising income or other financial assistance	**-**	
Grand Total	Rec: $250-$1,000 Competitive: $3,000+	

Cost Saving Ideas

Ok, all done with the accounting of money going out. Phew. Now let's figure out how to reduce or eliminate some of those expenses!

- Hand me downs from friends or family with older players

- Re-use or multipurpose gear you already have on hand. For example, for cold weather, you can use a warm thermal layer you already have rather than buying something baseball-specific.

- Secondhand shops or online sales of used equipment. These can be helpful for buying stuff you need at a discount. Some items – like gloves – may be even better secondhand, as they're nice and broken in already! But, as always, buyer beware to make sure whatever you're buying is still in decent shape. If you don't have family or friends to hand equipment down to, you can also sell stuff you're done with for a few bucks, perhaps to recycle the funds towards something new your player needs.

- Build it into gift giving. If/when family members ask what your player would like for birthdays or holidays, or when you're planning your own gifts for them, think of that new pair of sunglasses or batting gloves they need, or ask for gift cards to your favorite sporting goods store. Perhaps the big gift of the year is the new bat they've been dreaming of.

- Look for independent teams (vs. clubs) for competitive play. While there will still be expenses to cover, including uniforms, tournaments, travel, possible field rental for practice, etc., independent teams can cost thousands less per season than a club team.

- Some leagues give out coupons early in the season, often before or right when practice starts, for a sporting goods store. Coupon day can be a good time to stock up on anything your baseball player – or other family members! – may need.

- Look around for financial aid. Some leagues or clubs may offset some or all fees in cases of financial need and/or exceptional talent.

- And, of course, fundraising!

Team Fundraising

If finding ways to offset costs is a priority for your team, there are a variety of fundraising activities you can do as a group. A few ideas are included here, but the possibilities are limited only by your wild imagination! Often, more creative fundraising can be more successful, as it's a novelty for those being approached to donate/participate.

One note on fundraising philosophy. From my take-it-or-leave-it peanut gallery perspective, team fundraising should be targeted at bringing in OUTSIDE money. Meaning, from somewhere other than the players' parents. Fundraising takes time and energy - often scarce resources among moms in general and baseball moms in particular. And if the only people buying what we're selling is ourselves, so costs are just shifted rather than reduced, why bother? Really though.

Also, you'll want to be clear up front regarding which families are in and willing to help, and when. It can be frustrating to put a lot of time into planning a fundraiser and then have it fall apart with low participation. **If there isn't a lot of team-wide interest, structure fundraising to be individually driven for individual benefit** from the get go.

If you do fundraise as a group, where does the money go? **Your team will need to decide how the fundraised money is used, and you will want to be crystal clear that everyone's on the same page on this point in advance.**

Options include:

- It can all be pooled together and put in a lump sum toward the total team fees, so everyone's share is lowered by an equal amount. Perhaps the original total amount of team fees covering tournaments and coach travel was $10,000. If there are 10 players (for easy math), each family's original obligation would be $1,000. If you fundraise $1,000, the total would be reduced to $9,000, and each family's share would be reduced to $900.

- There can be an opt-out option. If there are families who are more financially comfortable and don't need the fundraising, they could anonymously opt out and the fundraised money could further reduce the fee share for the other families.

- Each player could have the money they fundraise applied directly toward their own team fees. So, if they sell x number of Super Bowl squares and x number of gift cards, that amount could directly reduce their family's share of fees, rather than being pooled together with other players.

A few ideas for fundraising are included here. They can be used directly, or as inspiration for something else new and fun!

Put Those Kids to Work!

This whole thing is for them anyway. It would do them good to have some skin in the game and may inspire a deeper appreciation of the investment in their opportunity to play.

- Car wash or snow shoveling - manual labor in exchange for donations to the team. Call it endurance or strength training.

- Sponsored volunteering - have them seek pledges or donations for the team, or their own fees, for each hour/afternoon/whatever they spend supporting a local community organization, picking up trash, or doing another team-organized service event. Some organizations have a minimum age for volunteers, so it may take a little legwork in advance to set something up. **But this is a win-win-win-win**. Your community is supported, the team benefits from a cost offset, and the kids can develop a heart for service to others, especially if it's framed in the right way for them in advance, so they understand why the service they're doing is important in the bigger picture. And of course, they may even have some fun spending time together away from the field! Volunteering together is a great team building activity whether there's a fundraising element or not.

Super Bowl / Really-Any-Game Squares

While this game/fundraiser is most popular around the Super Bowl, it could be done for a World Series game, the Stanley Cup final, a World Cup soccer game, or your favorite local sports team's game against their biggest rival. Any old game you choose.

- It can be done in person or online. The online option creates the largest potential pool of participants.

- There are all kinds of formulas and platforms you can use, from a snazzy online tool to a piece of paper with a hand-drawn grid on it. The grid will have ten rows and ten columns, for a total of 100 squares. Each axis of the grid will have numbers from 0-9 at the top and side of each

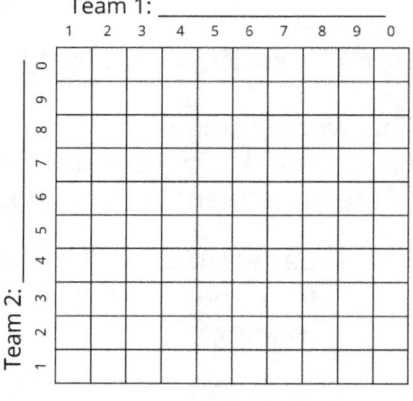

Super Bowl/Any Game Squares Example

Team 1: _____

Team 2: _____

row/column. The numbers can be in any order, and it may be best to add them after the squares are sold, but before the game, so it's random. One axis (top or side) is assigned to each team playing in your chosen game. The numbers correspond to the last digit in that team's score at the end of the game. For example, if the final score was 31-27, the winning square would be the one at the intersection of the "1" column or row for the first team and in the "7" row or column for the second team.

- People will purchase one or more squares - by self-selection or by random-assignment before the game starts - for a set price per square. Your team fundraising committee will decide what price seems reasonable per square. $1? $5? $10? The higher the price per square, the more money your team will make. But the harder you'll have to work to sell all of them.

- You'll decide how you want to structure your winnings. For example, you could say the winner will get 25% or 50% of the pot. If you're selling squares for $1 per square and have a 25% winner, the winner would get $25 and the team would get $75. At $10 per square, the winner would get $250 and the team would get $750. **Structure the price per square and winner percentage as you see fit**.

- Note - if you want to make sure there's a winner, it's important to sell out every square of the grid. Otherwise, there's a risk that nobody will win if the winning square is unbought. Although... you could structure winnings to be "x% of squares sold" and note in advance that if an unbought square is the winner, the team wins and gets the whole pot!

- Another option - if your team sells out all the squares on one grid super-fast with lots of time before the game, you could have a second grid, or more!

Restaurant Gift Cards

- Some restaurants sell gift cards to teams at less than face value to support area youth sports. The team can then sell them to others at face value, and put the difference in the team treasury. For example, if a restaurant sells a $50 gift card to the team for $25, when the team re-sells the gift card for $50, they'd keep the $25 difference.

- This can be a good option at times of year when you can advertise the gift cards as team-supporting gifts (perhaps before the winter holidays, or in the run up to Valentine's Day, etc.).

- If you do this option, I'd recommend getting pre-orders and payment from anyone who wants one. This way, you don't get stuck paying for gift cards you don't need or can't sell. You'll just need a good, transparent tracking system so everyone gets what they paid for.

Team Sponsorship by Local Businesses

- If your team has any control over the design of your jerseys or practice shirts, and/or if you have other items you'll use regularly in public at games like a banner or a team pop-up shade tent, you can look for local sponsors. In exchange for whatever amount of donation you think sounds reasonable, you can print their company logo on your team items. It's advertising for them, and cash for the team!

Auctioning a Basket of Donated Items

- You can seek donations of items from local businesses, and then auction it off all together as a fun basket. Consider having some kind of theme for the basket. You can have a silent (or out loud in person!) auction for the basket.

You'll want to set the starting bid for the basket (or each item, if you have good standalone donations) at a level that's helpful for the team but also still a good deal for the bidders, to incentivize them to want to bid and compete for it.

General Fund

- Just ask for straight cash. Might as well have a cut-to-the-chase option for anyone who is willing to help the team but doesn't want to buy squares or gift cards or baskets or butter-braids or to go to a specific local restaurant next Tuesday between 5:00 and 7:00 and mention the team. You can have your kid make a video explaining how much they love baseball and that their team is looking for donations to help keep the price of participating accessible for all players. Then send the video and a link for a payment collector for the team around to family members or baseball-loving friends who might be willing to donate an amount of their choosing.

- If there are families on the team who are more financially comfortable, they may make an anonymous donation to the team, which could reduce the share of fees for each family.

Fundraising Planner			
Date	Type	Estimated Value	Actual Value

Chapter 8
When Things Start to Get Serious: High School & Beyond

Youth baseball goes up to 14U. Some players who are on the younger side of their class in school may only play through 13U. After that, the players are in high school. I know, be still my heart. *Weren't we just playing tee-ball?! How did we get here already???* Some players may choose to hang up their cleats once they get to high school in favor of another sport or activity, with their time in youth baseball toggling over from daily experience to fond childhood memory. Others may dig in, with hopes to play through high school, in college, and, for a lucky few, beyond.

High School

High school baseball is a spring sport. Training will usually start after winter break, and games will run from March through May. After the school sports season wraps up, the high school team may continue to play together at some tournaments during summer break. Or, if the school team is done for the season, players may be encouraged to join another league or club team to extend playing time beyond the school season, which runs a little shorter than youth competitive seasons.

Your school may offer open houses or parent meetings near the end of 8th grade and/or early in their freshman year. These can be school-wide for all athletics and academics or sport-specific. Look for those and put them on the calendar so you and your player can learn more about what to expect at your school.

We're moms. We're - *obviously* - always here to support our kids, even as they grow taller than us. We'll always be present in the background to encourage our favorite player and to receive information intended for families. However, once the time comes for face time at the school, **your player should be encouraged to take the lead**. In fact, taking a few steps back should probably start years earlier. This helps our kids develop the confidence and responsibility to communicate with their coach. For those of us with shy kids, we may need to encourage them in advance to be ready to shake the high school coach's hand, introduce themselves, be ready to answer questions about their playing experience, and be prepared with a few questions they'd like to ask the coach about high school baseball. In a setting meant for parents we can, and of course should, be friendly, introduce ourselves, and ask questions. But it's (probably past) time for mom to take the back seat to our player in direct coach interaction.

Like all high school sports, baseball can be a big time commitment, with practices and/or games every day during pre-season training and the season. **Our players need to figure out how to manage their time efficiently** (yay, life skills!) to get all of their homework done in addition to team and other commitments they may have, like a part-time job.

Depending on the size of your high school, there may be different levels of competition and opportunity. A smaller school may have one baseball team. A larger school could have multiple levels, with perhaps a no-cut (everyone can play) Freshman team as well as Junior Varsity and Varsity teams for which spots may be more competitive.

Unlike youth teams where the team sizes are somewhat small to give everyone plenty of playing time, there may be two to four times the number of players on the team as the number of available positions on the field, especially if your high school is big. **Players really start competing for playing time in their spot since multiple kids on the team will be angling for the same position. The coach will know about their grades and their attitude, so both of those need to be as shiny and ready**

for inspection as their on-field performance. They will need to practice a lot. Like, a lot a lot, in their free time outside of the required team practice. They need to play on-point, and they need to get strong.

While they can start with some limited strength training as tweens, with a focus on body-weight exercises (push-ups, squats, etc.), weightlifting often starts in earnest in high school, if not a bit before. A general rule of thumb is that once they start puberty, it's safe(r) to start weightlifting. Of course, every kid is different. So, if this is your kid's desired path, asking about them lifting weights is a good question for your pediatrician once they turn 12 or 13. However, weightlifting should always be done with proper guidance, ideally with a coach or team trainer, at least until they learn the proper movements and techniques. Lifting weights the wrong way - over developing some muscle groups and under developing others, and/or not also working on flexibility to prevent muscles from becoming too tight - can set the stage for injury.

So, they make the team (yay!) and earn playing time (yay!). We get to keep watching them play. Extra yay! What next?

College Recruiting

There's a (kinda) long time between registering for 9th grade classes as a second-semester 8th grader and graduating from high school, and we never know how our kid's interests and goals may change over those years. However, **if they're entering high school with aspirations to continue playing baseball in college, it can be helpful to at least know some of the rules and general flow of college recruiting**. There are some great books, websites, and social media groups out there written/administered by former coaches or other experts in the field. They go into much more detail about the college athletic recruiting/scholarship process and can be helpful resources.

Current academic requirements and other eligibility info can be found at NCAA.org. While most of the NCAA Division 1 (D1) academic standards - the highest level - will overlap with high school graduation requirements, there could be some differences. So, **if your kid is thinking about playing college sports, they may want to consider NCAA core course requirements while mapping out what classes they want to take in high school**. They also may want to peek at the NCAA website during class registration season each year to check for any changes and adjust their academic plan accordingly. Note that some classes taken before high school could count towards required NCAA credits if they're included on their high school transcript - classes like Algebra 1 or Spanish 1 that may be high-school level but that some of these smarty-pants kids might take as an 8th grader. If a student decides along the way that they're not interested in playing sports in college, then they've perhaps had a slightly more rigorous education than they needed. We'll call that a momming win and carry on.

Typically, high school players won't try to get in front of college programs until at least the spring of their sophomore year. While it's *possible* to get in front of some colleges during a player's freshman year of high school, it's less typical and there's still time until they need to start venturing down the college road. Time to actually, you know, be a high schooler.

Some schools have rules limiting when they can begin to communicate with prospective recruits. For NCAA schools, Division 2 (D2) coaches can contact a student athlete starting June 15 after their sophomore year, and official visits to campuses can also begin at that time. D1 coaches can't contact a recruit until a bit later: August 1 between their sophomore and junior year. Athletes can begin official visits or other unofficial on-campus recruiting at D1 schools starting September 1 of their junior year. There are no restrictions on when coaches from D3, NAIA, or junior colleges can begin to contact players.

Different divisions of schools also have different rules governing the timing of recruitment-related visits and communication. The NCAA has certain periods of time each year when different types of recruiting are permitted to happen. There are calendars with the specific dates for different sports in the different NCAA divisions on their website. These are important to look up, as the periods are kind of sprinkled around the calendar and the specific dates will change a bit from year to year. The four types of recruiting periods for D1 and D2 schools are:

- Contact period - open doors for all types of communication and evaluation. Cumulatively, the contact period is about six months of time.

- Quiet period - in-person contact is only permissible on the college campus, not elsewhere. Cumulatively, there's a little less than five months of this period, making it close to, but a little less than, the amount of time in contact periods.

- Dead period - no in-person contact or evaluation, and no official or unofficial visits to the college campus. Cumulatively, there's about three weeks of this classification sprinkled throughout the year. Some of these periods also fall over holidays, like the Fourth of July.

- Recruiting Shutdown - no communication or contact of any kind. These periods fall over and around the Thanksgiving and Christmas holidays, so cumulatively it's a bit less than two weeks of time during the year.

This is a lot. Where do we start?

The college selection process can be overwhelming for any student. Layer on the possibility of college-level athletics, and it becomes even more complicated.

There are over 1,600 college baseball teams at institutions ranging from junior colleges to D1 universities, with about 200-500 schools in each category (NCAA D1, NCAA D2, NCAA D3, NAIA, and junior colleges).

Your student athlete may want to start by:

- Thinking about what kind of academic programs or majors

they are interested in.

- Thinking about where - geographically - they're interested in going. Perhaps venturing out to experience a new region, or staying closer to the comfort of home or family.

- Just taking a gander at maps of where different schools are located, looking at ranking lists of schools with academic programs they're interested in, and clicking through college websites as general exploration. Kind of just digitally wandering around.

- Thinking about their hoped-for college experience: Do they prefer a big or small school? Do they want the flexibility and opportunity to do things outside of sports, like studying abroad or other activities?

- If you live near a college or three, or find yourself near one while traveling with the family, consider spending a few hours exploring here and there. Your student athlete may not necessarily be interested in attending those particular schools, but it can give them a general feel for the difference between big and small schools, what different campuses can look like, etc.

- **Keeping a list of places they discover that they'd like to consider or learn more about**. It can be a long list! It can also be subdivided into different categories, like top tier favorites, second tier, and acceptable-if-they-have-a-great-offer. As they dig in to research the schools they're most interested in, **it may be helpful for them to build their list in a program like Sheets or Excel, to keep track of information for each school, including:**

  ◦ State

  ◦ City

  ◦ Division (D1, D2, D3, NAIA, JuCo)

- Size of school (# on-campus undergraduate students)

- Majors of interest offered

- National rankings in possible area(s) of study?

- GPA/SAT/ACT requirements

- Estimated tuition, fees, room and board, books, and other costs (For example, will they need to buy a plane ticket every time they come home to visit, or can they drive?)

- Baseball team info, perhaps including ranking within their division or nationally

- Coach/Program contact info

- Contact history (followed/following on social media, dates of emails/calls, application submitted)

- Visits to campus

- Important dates, like showcases/camps and their registration deadlines, college application deadlines, etc.

- Other notes of interest about academics, athletics, or the school in general

Once your player has their list, they may want to start reaching out to the coaching department at their schools-of-interest once allowed by their division. So, probably the summer before or fall of their junior year. **Junior year is Prime Time for self-promotion and establishing contact with potential college teams**. If there's a favorite school or several that your kid wants to get in front of early, they could look at attending a showcase or camp there during their sophomore year. However, if it's a D2 or D1 school, while they can attend and be seen, they'll need to remember that the coaches won't be able to actually talk to them about recruiting until June 15 or August 1 after their sophomore year ends, respectively.

Official visits are campus visits that are paid for, either completely or partially, by the school inviting the player to visit. They can include a campus tour, visiting a class, meeting with coaches, and possibly watching a game. At D1 schools at least, students are limited to one official visit per school. Unofficial visits could have a lot of the same elements as an official visit, but are not paid for by the school. Unofficial visits are unlimited.

When do offers start? **Verbal offers of roster slots or scholarships could come any time after contact between coach and player is allowed to begin.** However, offers are not necessarily final and official until it's written down and signed. Typically letters of intent are signed starting in November of a player's senior year for D1 and D2 schools, though this varies in other divisions.

Self-Marketing Tools

Your player will need some tools to capture and document their on-field successes, and to strut their stuff in a way that allows interested schools to see and follow them.

Some of this could happen in-person, with a player attending a camp or showcase hosted by a college they're interested in. This could also happen if a recruiter attends one of their games in person(!!!).

A lot of self-marketing happens virtually, due to the lower time and cost commitment.

- **Video**: They'll need at least one video capturing some highlights of them playing. It can be helpful to release updated videos with fresh content as time passes. These can be housed on a platform like YouTube or other social media.

- **Social media**: FieldLevel, Instagram, and X, formerly known as Twitter, seem to be the preferred platforms to connect with college coaches. While players should not tag schools or coaches in their posts, they should follow those schools and coaches and invite them to follow them back. Social media can be a good platform to regularly share videos, stats, metrics, and updated successes.

- **Email**: Players may reach out to coaches to express interest in their school and team. Ideally, they should address these emails to a coach identified as the recruiting coordinator on a college's website. These should be 1) short, sweet, and easy to read, 2) tailored to the specific school (not a copy/paste form letter), and 3) attention-grabbing stuff goes near the beginning. It should include links to video(s) and their social media presence to encourage ongoing connection.

  - It may be time for your student to open a (professional, not silly/inappropriate) email address outside of their school system, if they don't have one already. That way, their contact information can remain consistent after high school graduation.

Dreaming of a Scholarship?

According to thecoachingeducator.com, as of 2019, the average baseball scholarship was about $13,000. The highest was about $26,000 and the lowest was about $6,300. How far that will get you in covering tuition depends, of course, on the cost of the school.

So, how does that translate? According to NCSAsports.org, **college baseball coaches are allocated a certain number of full scholarships that can be divided among a certain number of players on their team**. The rules here vary depending on whether the team is NCAA D1, NCAA D2, NAIA, or a junior college. **NCAA D3 schools don't give athletic scholarships, and neither do Ivy League or Patriot League schools.**

Let's look at D1 schools as an example, with those being the 'top tier' schools that may come to mind first when thinking of college sports. D1 baseball teams can have a roster of 35 players and are allocated up to 11.7 scholarships for the team. You read that right; 11.7 full scholarships is the NCAA cap per team, and that amount may or may not be fully funded by a school's athletic department. The (maybe, if funded) 11.7 scholarships can then be divided among up to 27 players, with each of those chosen players getting at least a 25% scholarship. Full-ride baseball scholarships are rare due to the already-low player-to-scholarship ratio. The remaining eight players on the team (35 on the roster - 27 receiving some amount of scholarship = 8) are walk-ons and play without a scholarship, though they may earn one in a future year. Most baseball scholarships are committed for one year at a time. So, whether or not a player will continue to receive the athletic scholarship portion of their financial assistance likely depends upon their performance from year to year, as well as other existing or incoming competition for a piece of the scholarship pie. Yeah, yikes.

However, **athletic scholarships are separate from and can be added to other financial assistance, including need-based, academic-based, and others**. So, partial scholarships, while perhaps not what's dreamed of, can still help chip away at the tuition bill, if the player can get one. Also, while your player may have D1 dreams, scholarships (and roster slots) are certainly available, and perhaps easier to land, at other levels of colleges. Ultimately, the best choice of a college is likely found at the intersection of a student-athlete's interest in their academic programs, financial aid offerings, and athletic opportunities. With, of course, a little input from their gut feelings and preferences.

Dreaming of The Show?

Nobody's here to crush dreams. A... few... of these kids will indeed walk out under the major league lights, and hear the crack of their bat ignite an explosion of cheering that roars through a stadium.

We don't know who will have their dream come true. But perhaps some perspective.

According to the NCAA, there are about 482,700 total high school baseball players annually. About 7.5% of those high school players become the next batch of about 36,000 total annual baseball players at NCAA and NAIA schools, which are 4-year colleges. There are additional players at junior colleges, or JuCos, which are 2-year schools. Each year, the MLB now drafts a little over 600 players. Until 2019, they drafted over 1,200 players each year, with historically about two-thirds of draftees coming from four-year colleges, and the remainder coming from junior colleges, high school, or other sources. Also, historically, about 75% of those drafted ended up signing some level of professional baseball contract, almost always to play with a minor league team.

There are 120 full-season minor league teams across the United States and Canada, as well as Rookie leagues that play in Arizona, Florida, and the Dominican Republic during the summer. Each of the 30 major league teams has four affiliated minor league teams as part of its organization, one in each of the four minor league divisions: Single-A, High-A, Double-A, and Triple-A, with Triple-A being the highest level. For example, The Colorado Rockies organization includes the Triple-A Albuquerque Isotopes, the Double-A Hartford Yard Goats, the High-A Spokane Indians, and the Single-A Fresno Grizzlies. Typically, draftees will begin their career on a minor league team, and the parent major league organization will call up the strongest players to play in the bigs. Or they may send major league players down to the minors if they are underperforming or if they need to recuperate after an injury.

In March 2023, minor league players did well in negotiations with the MLB, significantly increasing pay for players. Previously, pay for minor leaguers was famously low, sometimes even below the federal minimum wage. As of 2023, **minimum** salaries increased from $4,800 to $19,800 in the Rookie league and from $17,500 to $35,800 for players in Triple-A, with the other divisions having similar increases between those levels. Those amounts are the league minimums; players may make (a lot) more than that, and may also receive signing bonuses. Minor league players also get other benefits during the season to supplement their salary, including housing, meals, health care, tuition assistance, and per diem.

Minor league play could be a fun opportunity! Players in the lower divisions may still find themselves mowing lawns in the offseason to make ends meet, but they get paid (a bit) to play the game they love. If nothing else, it could be a fun experience for a few years before moving on to a "real job". And, a minor league player's dream is still alive, with hopes of getting picked up by a major league team to play on the big stage... where the minimum annual salary of $740,000, as of 2024, is in a whole different universe.

Of course, the likelihood of even a draftee seeing some action in the major league is... low. And it depends a lot on when in the draft they are selected. According to baseballamerica.com[1] , between 1981 and 2010, 17.6% of all drafted players ended up making it to the majors. However, the chances were much better for those drafted in the first round, with close to 75% of them eventually making it. That dropped off to about 40% by the third round and continued to tail off after that. The number of players drafted annually during the 1981-2010 timeframe ranged from 1,263 to 1,740, with an average of 1,474 each year.

How many rounds of the draft are there, you may ask? Currently, 20. Prior to 2019, there were 40 or more. Gah. Gah for there being fewer draftees now - a bit over 600 annually. And gah that there are still 20 (!!) rounds of the draft, when the chances of playing in the majors tank after about the second or third round. So, with fewer players being drafted now, perhaps the percentage of drafted minor leaguers making it to the show will increase?

For now, based on available numbers, a bit of educated logical leaping, and some pixie dust - *sharpens pencil, carries the one...* - about 0.054% of high school players and 0.719% of college players

---

1. https://www.baseballamerica.com/stories/how-many-mlb-draftees-make-it-to-the-majors/

eventually play in the major league in a moderately meaningful capacity. So, out of 10,000 high school players, about 5.4 advance to the majors, and out of 1,000 college players, about 7.2 advance. It's a lot better than the chances of winning a lottery jackpot... But, for those who do clear the in-itself-significant hurdle to play in college after playing in high school, they should probably make sure they're studying and building a solid Plan B career path given the extremely high likelihood that their future salary will come from somewhere other than the MLB.

Chapter 9
Tips, Translations, & Fun!

And finally, here's everything else. All the random stuff that's important, helpful to, and fun for baseball moms, but that doesn't need its own chapter. Like the junk drawer of the book. Just better organized?

The White Pants

There's probably some historical or traditional reason for baseball pants to (usually) be white. A decision clearly made by someone not doing the laundry after a game played sliding around in grass and red dirt. Every once in a while you may get lucky with darker pants in your kid's uniform. But, unless they're *really* dark, they're probably still going to need some laundry TLC, too.

For the player, having dirty pants is, of course, a badge of honor at the end of the game: proof of playing time and hard work while on the field. But they need to be cleaned up and reset as a blank canvas before the next game, when they'll be made into a badge again. And again.

There are, certainly, different strategies you can use to tackle this laundry challenge. You could try to just throw them in the washer with a regular load and hope for the best. I wouldn't blame you. Cleaning baseball pants is a pain in the ass. It may work sometimes, especially when kids are younger and play is less aggressive. Once dirt and grass really gets ground into the fabric, though, the pants will need some extra work to clean them up.

My favorite method:

- First, rinse off all the loose dirt with a hose or in a sink until the water starts to run fairly clean.

- Then the magic: hand scrub the extra-dirty spots with Fels-Naptha. You heard me. Push up those sleeves. This is an old-fashioned bar of laundry soap invented by wizards. It works better than any other fancy stain spray or soak I've tried. Wet the bar and scrub it directly onto the stained spots to work up a good lather. Don't worry about the yellow color of the soap - it'll wash out. Then, scrub the fabric against itself. Rinse a bit. How does it look? Repeat as necessary on tough spots, or move on to the next one.

- Use this same process on the jersey shirt for any stains there as well, but pants are getting all the attention here because they're usually so much worse.

- Then, just throw them into the washer with regular laundry detergent and wash as normal.

  - My friend and baseball mom mentor who is an extra-enthusiastic Fels-Naptha lover also grates up some of the bar of soap with a cheese grater and throws it into the washer with the load. I'm usually too lazy for this step, but it does give an extra cleaning boost if you need it.

- Thou shalt not dry the baseball pants. I mean, you can in a pinch if you have a game in a couple of hours and forgot to wash the uniform until this morning. But, if you can, try to avoid putting them in the dryer. In all likelihood, there may be a little lingering stubborn dirt or grass on the pants. Air drying allows you another go at removing more of that stain in a few days when you're doing this again, rather than baking it into the fabric for all time as dryers like to do.

Some of our baseball friends use other tactics. One stops by a manual car wash - the kind with the hand sprayer - and sprays the pants down with the high pressure wash. Similarly, some use a power washer at home. I haven't tried either of these methods, but it sounds fun and they swear by it. Others prefer to soak or spray with other products, including but not limited to Zout, Borax, Dawn Powerwash, and/or bleach.

I still stand on my Fels-Naptha hill.

Laundry Nirvana = passing the buck to your favorite baseball player. When they get to be old enough, definitely by 12-13 but maybe younger, it's time to empower the next generation with some laundry knowledge and hands-on training.

- Teach your kid the Fels-Naptha routine described above, or whatever preferred method you land on.

- Pour yourself a beverage of choice and enjoy it while you watch them work on their own pants.

- Pat yourself on the back for teaching them some important life skills and personal responsibility. And ridding yourself of a ridiculous chore, because you don't want to do that shit. Cheers!

Game Day Food

Games can be fun evening, weekend, or travel events. And at every fun event you need good food. Especially if you're going to be there all day so everyone isn't starving to death. **The goal with game day food is for it to be tasty (obviously), low-maintenance, and easily packable.** Isn't eating out or driving thru somewhere easier? You betcha. But for the times when you're tired of fast food, saving pennies, trying to eat healthier, or don't want to miss any action in back-to-back games, you may want to pack your own. The sky is really the limit here, and you can bring whatever you feel up to, have on hand, and your crew likes. But if you're looking for a few ideas to get started - or to switch things up! - here are some:

Breakfast

- **Breakfast burritos**: For something hearty, a favorite in our house is breakfast burritos. We'll make the meat and potato part of the filling the night before, quickly reheat it in the morning, scramble up some eggs, put it in tortillas with cheese and some sauce/gravy, and roll them up in foil. It's easy to eat in the car, for the player at least. Or, wrapped in a towel, will stay pretty warm for you and any fellow spectators to enjoy after arrival. Mix and match elements as you like and write names on the foil if everyone likes something different.
  ~ large tortillas
  ~ frozen hash browns
  ~ meat of choice (or not): breakfast sausage, chorizo, bacon, and/or diced ham (you get to skip the pre-cooking step if you just dice up a stack of deli ham)
  ~ scrambled eggs (or not)
  ~ cheese (or not)
  ~ some kind of sauce/gravy: For more traditional burritos use a green chile sauce (like the Stinkin' Good brand or whatever your grocery store stocks in the freezer section). For a more "country-style" flavor, or if green chili isn't common in your region, we also like white gravy. The packet stuff is good enough and can also be made the day prior and reheated.
  ~ other add-ins could include diced avocado, tomatoes, beans, or rice

- **Breakfast sandwiches**: If you have time in the morning, these only take a few minutes to make fresh if all you have to cook is an egg. Or they can be put together the night before, stored in the fridge, and put in the microwave for a few seconds to warm them up. If your crew wants a more high-maintenance meat like bacon or sausage, you could make that part ahead to save time in the morning. Further shortcut: keep some store-bought sandwiches in the freezer. Mix and match from:

~ carb of choice toasted & buttered: sliced bread, English muffin, roll, pita pocket, or bagel
~ egg (or not)
~ meat of choice (or not): sausage patty, bacon, ham, and/or salmon/lox
~ cheese (or not)
~ other toppings as you prefer: avocado, tomato, onion, cucumber, cream cheese, or spinach

- **Grab & Go**: for lighter eaters, or when you're extra short on time
  ~ protein or granola bar
  ~ fruit
  ~ yogurt
  ~ cottage cheese
  ~ toast with a nut butter
  ~ muffin/pastry – If you're trying to get more protein (vs. sugar) into your player before the game, you could Pinterest or Google search for a healthy recipe you think you can trick your kid into eating, one with their favorite flavors, then make a batch ahead of time.
  ~ breakfast bowl: Prep your favorite ingredients from the inside of a burrito or sandwich into a container; throw it in the cooler with a fork (don't forget the fork...) and eat it later.

Lunch/Dinner

- **The Sandwich**: Our family has a love/exhausted relationship with sandwiches. We love them because they're easy, tasty, portable, can be made a bit ahead of time, and everyone can personalize theirs how they like it. We're exhausted of them when we've eaten a hundred million by the end of the season and never want to see one again. Tolerance for sandwiches will last longer if the genre and ingredients are regularly and substantially mixed up.
  ~ Carb of choice: sliced bread, roll, bun, bagel, pita pocket, or tortilla

~ Spread(s) of choice: mayo, mustard, PB&J, hummus, cream cheese, ranch, honey mustard, oil and vinegar, tzatziki, green chili, drizzle of hot sauce, etc.
~ Meat(s) (or not): turkey, chicken, ham, roast beef, bacon, salami, pepperoni, etc.
~ Cheese (or not): slice of cheddar, American, Colby jack, pepper jack, etc.; or a sprinkle of queso fresco or pieces of fresh mozzarella, etc.
~ Veggie(s) (or not): tomato, lettuce, spinach, avocado, cucumber, bell pepper, banana pepper, pickles, onion, etc.

- **Wraps**: These recipes are differentiated from sandwiches only because the ingredients are more intermingled; the filling works best in a tortilla or something else that limits spillage, like a pita pocket. To avoid the tortilla/pita getting soggy (gross), consider putting the filling in a container and keeping it in the cooler (with a large spoon). Spoon it onto the tortilla/pita whenever you and your crew are ready to eat. For any with chicken, consider get some pre-cooked rotisserie meat from the deli to save time. Or throw some raw chicken in a slow cooker or pressure cooker in advance; it can do its thing in the background while you do other not-cooking stuff and will keep in the fridge for a few days. You can get creative with wraps/pockets, but a few of our go-to ideas are:
~ cooked chicken (diced or shredded), diced tomatoes, diced avocados, and ranch dressing. Stir together. Add some lettuce when putting in the tortilla for whoever likes that.
~ a more traditional chicken salad: cooked chicken (diced or shredded), mayo, lemon juice, and black pepper; add in sliced almonds, celery, and/or halved grapes
~ burrito-style with any combo of: cooked taco meat (chicken, pork, or beef), beans, rice, tomatoes, avocados, cheese, sour cream, and salsa or chili. Stir together. Add lettuce at serving time for anyone who wants it.
~ salad: any of the above "fillings" could be dolloped onto lettuce if you prefer to eat it as a salad. Put a handful of

lettuce into a separate container/bowl and throw it in the cooler. Again, with a fork.

- **Hot Dogs**: I mean, it is baseball. Heat up some hot dogs or sausages at home, put them in buns with preferred adornments, wrap in foil individually, and off you go. Or, if you want to bring the party to the field, bring a camping grill, pack(s) of hot dogs, sausages, and/or burgers, as well as buns and fixin's, and cook them up on site between or after games.

- Throw in some fruit, veggies, chips, and/or, for the player at least, some extra protein. Maybe a sweet treat for anyone not on the team - players can have theirs after the game.

Snacks

- **Long-lasting stuff**: Consider having **a bag that non-perishable baseball snacks live in for the season**. You'll need to replenish as things as they disappear, but at least you won't have to start from scratch before each game. Maybe keep a list pinned to the inside of the bag or in a pocket with all the staples, so that when you forget what was in there and needs to be refilled you have a reference. A few ideas:
  ~ protein/granola bars
  ~ beef jerky
  ~ trail mix or mixed nuts *(perhaps check that nobody on the team has severe allergies before sending anything with nuts into the dugout)*
  ~ popcorn/pretzels/chips/crackers
  ~ apple sauce packets
  ~ dried fruit
  ~ fruit snacks
  ~ cookies/candy

- **Stuff for the cooler**:
  ~ fruit / veggies

~ string cheese / sliced cheese
~ hummus / guacamole, or another easy dip for veggies or crackers
~ Lunchables / 'charcuterie' packs with meat, cheese, and crackers, or just throw stuff in Ziplocs/containers if you have all the elements

Glossary of Oft-Heard Baseball Terms

Baseball is famous for having dictionary's worth of slang and funny phrases. A few are defined here, but there are so many more!

Things People Say at Games

- "Heads!" = Ok, this one's not all that unique. But be aware that balls are **constantly** being hit over fences at games. Responsible spectators will repeatedly yell, "Heads!" as a warning for people at nearby fields or anyone in the vicinity. When you hear this regular refrain, **do not look up**. Unless you want to see the errant ball just before it hits you in the face. Rather, brace yourself, or maybe duck and cover.

- "Wear it." = encouragement to the batter to get hit by pitch and not step out of the way if the pitcher is throwing inside. Oof.

- "Eat it." = usually intended for a defending player to "eat"/accept that a stolen base has occurred, and not throw the ball at the last second to try to get them out. When this is said, it's usually judged to be futile/too late/too risky to try for an out at that moment. A hasty overthrow could result in more stolen bases and/or a score.

- "Flush it." = Forget about/mentally flush whatever just happened and move on.

- "Four! Four! Four!" = When the catcher (usually) or another player is yelling four, they're not warning about an incoming golf ball. They're calling for the ball to be thrown to home plate (a.k.a. - the "fourth" base) for an out.

- "Balls in! Coming down!" = The catcher yells this to indicate that the brief pitcher/field warm-up, which happens just prior to each half inning, is over. The rest of the fielders need to return their practice balls to the dugout (Balls in!) and the catcher is going to practice a throw to 2nd base (Coming down!).

- "Ribbie." = RBI = Runs Batted In statistic. Someone may say "ribbie" as a consolation to a batter who is out on the play, but whose at bat resulted in a teammate scoring.

- "He's hosed!" = A player is "hosed" when they are recently or imminently out while attempting to steal due to a strong throw by the defense. Relatedly, a "hose" is a strong throwing arm. i.e. "He has a hose!"

- Non-verbal signals/signs = You may see a coach wiping his forehead, touching his nose, swiping a hand down his arm, and/or making a series of other gestures. The coach is giving offensive (often from the third base side) or defensive (from in or near the dugout) signs to the team. Each team uses different gestures to mean different things. It's like their own secret code. The catcher will also use discreet finger gestures to suggest a type of pitch to the pitcher; they may be passing this on from a coach who also made a signal or deciding on their own. Some signs or signals are subtle and easily missed. Others are more obvious.

Nouns, Verbs, and Adjectives

- Around the horn

  ○ 1) A double or triple play that starts with the third baseman, who throws to second, who throws to first.

Or,

- ○ 2) When the infielders throw the ball around to each other in celebration after an out, if there isn't anyone on base.

- Bag = base; can be used for 1st, 2nd, or 3rd base

- Behind the dish = location where the catcher and umpire hang out between home plate and the backstop

- Blue = the umpire. Because back in the day their traditional uniforms were blue. Sometimes they still are blue, but not always.

- Bullpen = where pitchers warm up; may also refer to the collective group of pitchers on a team

- Bush league = amateur play or behavior. A term often thrown around when someone is deemed to be playing dirty or without class.

- Can of corn = a fly ball that's easily caught by outfielders

- Choke up = gripping the bat higher up on the handle for better control

- The Corners = 1st and 3rd bases

- Dime = a ball thrown precisely on target; a term only used by players, not moms. We are not cool enough and will ruin the term. Can also be a verb. i.e. "He dimed it!"

- Dinger = home run

- Dot = same as dime

- Dish = home plate (plate = dish = yeah)

- Ducks on the pond = two or three players on base. i.e. "There's ducks on the pond. Bring them home!"

- Grand slam = a home run when the bases are loaded, earning four total runs on the hit

- High cheese = a fastball on the upper edge of the strike zone

- Hole = any gap between fielders, but particularly in the infield and most often referring to the area between shortstop and third base.

  - Unrelatedly, someone is "in the hole" if they're currently third in line to hit, after the current batter and the player "on deck".

- Inside pitch = thrown on the side of the plate closer to the batter

- Meatball = a pitched ball that a batter can easily hit; delicious, juicy, and satisfying

- On deck = next up to bat

- Outside pitch = thrown on the side of the plate away from the batter

- Passed Ball vs. Wild Pitch = think of this as pitcher moms vs. catcher moms, respectively. Both of these are pitched balls that get behind the catcher. A passed ball is a mistake by the catcher, when the pitch was catchable, but they missed it. A wild pitch is a mistake by the pitcher, when the throw was so off target it wasn't reasonably catchable by the catcher.

- The Show = Major League Baseball

- Squeeze play = a squeeze play is when a batter bunts rather than hits the ball, trying to bring in a runner at third base to score. It's a risky play and often results in an out (a "suicide squeeze"), but a coach may weigh the benefit of a possible run greater than the risk of an out in some situations.

- Tunnels = long and narrow partitions of space in a training facility, usually separated by nets. Used to contain balls when practicing throwing or hitting.

  - If you're hanging out near tunnels while your kid is practicing, stay at least 2-3 feet back from every net. Balls are coming in hot, and can hit anyone standing too close within the net's range of motion.

- Uncle Charlie = a curve ball

- Warning track = the area of dirt bordering the outfield fence

- Whiff = a swing of the bat that only hits air; a swing & miss for a strike

- Worm burner = a high-speed grounder

Honors

- Hitting for the cycle = when a batter hits a single, a double, a triple, and a homerun in one game

- Triple Crown = when a player leads their league in batting average, home runs, and runs batted in (RBI) during the same season

- Pitching Triple Crown = when a pitcher leads their league in wins, strikeouts, and earned run average (ERA)

Movie Night

In our house we like to celebrate the start of baseball season by watching baseball movies! There are literally hundreds of movies - you could watch them year-round. But we have some favorites that make regular appearances on family movie nights.

The Sandlot
~ 1993, PG
~ Scotty Smalls, who knows nothing about baseball, is the new kid who just moved to town. He's taken under the wing of Benny, a modest and kind neighbor kid who leads a ragtag pick-up baseball team. A monster with a reputation for eating kids, "The Beast", lives beyond the sandlot's outfield fence. Adventure ensues.
~ Takeaway quotes: *"You're killing me, Smalls!"* and *"For-ev-er."*

Major League
~ 1989, R, Tom Berenger, Charlie Sheen
~ Washed-up catcher Jake Taylor (Berenger) and others are recruited by the Cleveland Indians in an attempt to assemble a terrible team on purpose. The owner wants the team to come in last place so she can move it from Ohio to Florida.
~ While this is rated R, it's not **as** bad as some others. Your call on whether it's ok for your kiddos. There are a few sexual references, but not as many as Bull Durham, at least in our read of it.
~ Takeaway quotes: *"It's very bad to take Jobu's rum. Very bad."* or *"This guy threw at his own kid in a father-son game."* or *"Juuuuust a bit outside."* or *"Are you trying to say Jesus Christ can't hit a curveball?"* and *"Forget the curveball, Ricky. Give him the heater."* It's basically a goldmine of quotable one-liners.

A League of Their Own (when I have the remote; the kids do like it, though)
~ 1992, PG, Geena Davis, Tom Hanks, Madonna
~ During WWII, while all the male baseball players were fighting abroad, owners stood up a women's baseball league. Dottie Hinson (Davis) and her sister are recruited to play for Jimmy Dugan's (Hanks) team. Dugan is an ex-MLB player with a drinking problem who isn't fighting due to a (drinking-related) injury.
~ Takeaway quote: *"There's no crying in baseball!"*

42
~ 2013, PG-13, Chadwick Boseman, Harrison Ford
~ The story of Jackie Robinson (Boseman), who broke the MLB color barrier as the first African American to play. Important history and a great movie.

~ Takeaway quotes: *Reporter: "Whatcha gonna do if one of these pitchers throws for your head?" Robinson: "I'll duck."* and *"Maybe tomorrow we'll all wear 42, that way they won't tell us apart."*

The Bad News Bears
~ PG - the 1976 version with Walter Matthau has better ratings, but we like the 2005 version with Billy Bob Thornton, too.
~ Former minor league player and current day-drinking pool cleaner/bug exterminator Morris Buttermaker (Matthau/Thornton) agrees to coach a little league team. Day 1 of practice reveals that the players have virtually no baseball or athletic talent.
~ Takeaway quotes: *"This is not a democracy! It's a dictatorship! Now get your stuff and get your asses out on the field!"*

Bull Durham
~... is great, but not for young ones. Watch sometime after they're in bed.
~ 1988, R, Kevin Costner, Susan Sarandon, Tim Robbins
~ Crash Davis (Costner), a great catcher who's played almost perpetually in the minor league, is recruited by the Durham Bulls to mentor a new pitcher (Robbins). Annie Savoy (Sarandon) has a monogamous affair with one player on the Bulls each season and is a mentor in her own way. Love triangle and baseball.
~ Takeaway quotes: *"He hit the f*cking bull. Guy gets a free steak!"* and *"Strikeouts are boring. Besides that, they're fascist."* and *"The rose goes in the front, big guy."*

Moneyball
~2011, PG-13, Brad Pitt, Jonah Hill
~ Billy Beane (Pitt), the General Manager of the Oakland A's, is struggling to put together a winning team on a shoestring budget. Peter Brand (Hill) is a recent Yale grad with a unique take on player potential using statistics. Much to the confusion of the rest of the A's organization, Beane hires Hill to help identify and bring in undervalued players. Some of the premise may go over young ones heads, but it could add perceived value to math homework. Based on a true story.
~ Takeaway quotes: *"There are rich teams and there are poor teams.*

Then there's 50 feet of crap. Then there's us." and *"How can you not be romantic about baseball?"*

Field of Dreams
~ 1989, PG, Kevin Costner, James Earl Jones
~ Ray Kinsella (Costner) starts hearing a voice giving cryptic instructions, such as "If you build it, he will come." "It" is a baseball field in the middle of his Iowa corn farm, and "he" is Shoeless Joe Jackson, part of the 'Chicago 8' White Sox players accused of throwing the 1919 World Series in a gambling venture and banned from the game. In his quest to understand the messages, Kinsella seeks out former-writer and now-recluse Terence Mann (Jones) for guidance. The whole premise is a little weird, but it's a classic so has to go on the list. Kind of like making your kids ride "It's a Small World" at Disneyland on principle. You have to do it.
~ Takeaway quote: *"If you build it, they will come."*

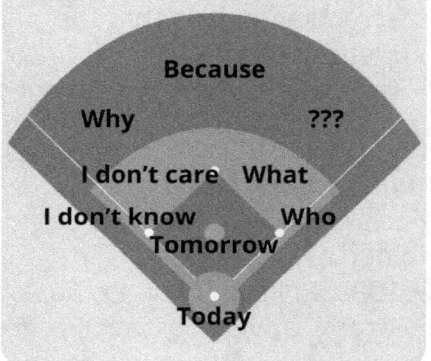

Who's on First?

It's old. But it's a classic. Pull up the Abbott and Costello skit *Who's on First?* on YouTube or your smart speaker for a listen and a chuckle.

Some interesting documentary-style ones:

Facing Nolan
~ 2022, TV-14
~ The story of Nolan Ryan, baseball badass hailing from Texas.

It Ain't Over
~ 2022, PG
~ The story of Yogi Berra, Yankees legend and source of funny/quirky/famous quotes like, *"It ain't over 'til it's over,"* and *"Baseball is 90% mental. The other half is physical."*

The Battered Bastards of Baseball
~ 2014, R

~ Did you know actor Kurt Russell's dad started a baseball team in 1973?

Get in the Game

And that's a wrap! My at bat is over and you're on deck. While there's (always!) more to learn about this crazy game, it's time to load up, roll out, and enjoy your own baseball adventure with your kiddo. You're ready. There will be home runs and hitting slumps, sunny blue skies and rainouts, laughter with new friends and grumpy car rides home. Take it for what it offers. It's a game and it's (usually) fun! It's low-stakes failure and frustration, but it's also learning, breakthroughs, and celebration. It's life. And at the end of the day, it's time together. Enjoy the game!

Acknowledgements

The best thing about this baseball journey is all the people we've walked the road with – the old friends and the new.

Thanks to Beth who first lured our family away from soccer field exclusivity to try something new.

Thanks to Coach Chad and Laurie for SO much! For helping our family develop a love for the game. For helping both our kids get better. For bridging us into and teaching us the ways of competitive baseball land. For paving the way to great teams for both of our kids at least three times. And for generally being some of our favorite humans.

Thanks to all the great coaches our boys have learned from over the years. From Coach Jeremy, a maestro at managing a tee-ball practice and keeping 5-year-olds engaged, learning, and having fun. To Coach Scoty G and Coach K, who gave our kid a shot at competitive play and who we've been fortunate to travel around with for four years. I hope you see yourselves in my description of what a great coach looks like, because the two of you inspired it. You even tolerate a crazy mom writing a book about baseball – thanks Scot for taking the time to read it and provide feedback, and Kevin for sharing your knowledge about stats. And to Peyton, Dennis, and so many other coaches in between and yet to come – thank you for doing what you do for your teams. You are more important in their lives than you know.

Thanks to all our extended baseball family members, and of course my fellow baseball moms! You've become some of our dearest friends, both at and away from the field. From commiserating on the weather or hitting slumps to supporting and cheering on each other's kids like our own. From late-night sing-alongs at the parents' house in Cooperstown to the mom text group planning team dinners, arranging carpools, and debating which color socks the boys wear tomorrow. We're so grateful to have you in our lives. Much love to you all.

Thanks to Tiffani for all of your encouragement and support as I gave this writing thing a shot. You were full of all the confidence I didn't have in myself.

And, of course, to my family – Mark, Eddie, and Tommy. Thank you for tolerating me tiptoeing around the house and clicking away at the keyboard starting around 4:00 a.m. for months. For answering my questions about the game. For keeping my secret that I was writing a book, allowing me the mental freedom to actually do it. For your support during this project. For filling my heart up every day. I love you all. I'm the luckiest.

About the author

Heather Dirck grew up in Colorado and still calls it home. After earning degrees in journalism and strategic communication from the University of Missouri she began her career, which she's dedicated to outreach for AmeriCorps NCCC, an awesome national service program. Back in high school, Heather thought she might write a book one day. A few decades later, she got around to it. She lives with her amazing family: her husband, her two sons (her favorite baseball players), two golden retrievers, and a cat who thinks he's a golden retriever. Baseball mom since 2015.